working woman's pregnancy

working woman's pregnancy

Hilary Boyd

Medical consultant: Dr Richard Porter F.R.C.O.G.

Legal consultant: Katie Wood – Maternity Alliance

Working Woman's Pregnancy
Hilary Boyd

Published in 2001 by Mitchell Beazley,
an imprint of Octopus Publishing Group Ltd,
2–4 Heron Quays, London, E14 4JP

ISBN 1 84000 349 9
A CIP catalogue copy of this book is available from the British Library.

Executive Editor	Vivien Antwi
Executive Art Editor	Kenny Grant
Project Editor	Michelle Bernard
Art Editor	Christine Keilty
Editor	Claire Musters
Design	Cobalt Information Design
Illustrations	David Ashby
Picture research	Jenny Faithfull
Production	Catherine Lay
Proofreader	Clare Hacking
Indexer	Hilary Bird
Medical consultant	Dr Richard Porter F.R.C.O.G.
Legal consultant	Katie Wood – Maternity Alliance

Printed and bound by Toppan Printing Company, China
Typeset in Perpetua and Vectora

contents

Having a baby is probably the most exciting thing you will ever experience and pregnancy should be a process that you are able to enjoy and share with all those around you. The first time your baby moves and the first scan that shows your baby's tiny outline are unforgettable moments.

Women are no longer coy about pregnancy; they wear clothes that reveal their expanding shape, talk about their experiences openly and expect the men in their lives to take an active role. But there is one arena in which many women allow pregnancy to take a back seat, and that is in the workplace. With such a high proportion of women now working throughout their pregnancy, and then planning to combine motherhood with a career, it is ridiculous that pregnancy is so often overshadowed by work. This book hopes to change your view on your position so that you can truly enjoy both your pregnancy and your work, and successfully combine the two. It will also give you the confidence to put yourself first during this unique time.

By understanding your rights and learning how to make careful plans, you should be able to fit everything into your work schedule from antenatal appointments and classes, ultrasound scans and buying equipment for your baby to keeping yourself fit.

This book also explains the complications of maternity leave and discusses in detail the difficult decision about whether to return to work or be a full-time mother. Until very recently, women have taken the whole burden of childcare onto their own shoulders, but times are changing, and society is becoming increasingly parent-friendly. This has enabled women to ask to work differently, in ways that allow them to manage both family and home without having to be superwoman.

As a woman in the 21st century you can look forward to a happy, healthy pregnancy within the structure of your working life. So make sure that you take the time to enjoy it all.

your pregnancy

timing and taking care

Some babies are unplanned, but still very much wanted and loved. However, today, with more efficient methods of contraception, many of us decide well in advance when we would like to start a family, so that we can get fit, sort out our home and finances and plan how we are going to make the transition from couple to family in the easiest and most straightforward manner.

It is obviously better to be able to plan when you get pregnant, and some jobs lend themselves to you being pregnant at certain times of the year, such as teaching, when having a baby at the beginning of the summer holidays is most convenient. But babies have a habit of turning up when they choose, and if you try to allow your job to dictate when you should get pregnant you will only cause yourself unnecessary stress when it doesn't happen exactly when you want it to. And you shouldn't put off having a baby too long because of job considerations, because you may discover that you are not as fertile as you used to be.

There are financial considerations that mean it is sensible to plan your pregnancy to your best advantage. You might want to save some money to help with the initial outlay of having a baby, or may want to put off trying for a baby until you have been employed for six months continuously in your present job, to ensure that you are entitled to extended maternity leave. You may also want to wait until you have received a proposed promotion before taking time out to have children.

Sometimes, despite the most meticulous forward thinking, we can find ourselves dealing with an unplanned pregnancy. But don't panic if this happens to you, as nine months is plenty of time to sort things out. It just means that you will have to make your decisions about work and finance quickly rather than planning them in advance. The most important thing, especially if you are working, is to enlist the support of those around you, both at work and at home, right from the start. Pregnancy can be a tiring business but, with support and careful planning, you should be able to continue to work comfortably until you choose to begin your maternity leave.

EATING NUTRITIOUSLY

You do not have to start eating for two as soon as you find out you are pregnant. If you ensure that your diet is well-balanced you will be providing for both you and your baby's nutritional needs. Here are some tips about which foods to eat and those to avoid:

- Eat plenty of food that is high in fibre and low in fat and sugar, such as wholegrain bread, pasta and rice.
- Eat lean meat, fish, eggs, nuts etc to provide protein.
- Eat at least five servings of fresh fruit and vegetables a day.
- Avoid alcohol and junk food.

time chart for pregnancy

This chart gives you an overview of your pregnancy, including when appointments and tests will happen. It also advises you on the steps you should be taking at various stages. Refer to the 'week-by-week guide' on pages 20–65 for further details.

Weeks 1–7

- Visit your doctor or midwife as soon as you suspect you are pregnant.
- Study your company's maternity policy.
- Give up smoking and limit alcohol intake.
- Check your immunity to Rubella.
- Get Form FW8 for free prescriptions and dental care during pregnancy and for 12 months afterwards.

Weeks 8–12

- Tell your employer that you are pregnant and think about when you want to start your maternity leave.
- Stock up on low-fat snacks at work to avoid morning sickness.
- You will have your first appointment with your midwife or GP.
- Buy yourself a new bra.
- Nuchal translucency scan can be done now if advised (chorionic villus sampling may be suggested too).

Weeks 13–16

- Inform your work about what maternity leave you have decided upon and when your antenatal appointments are.
- You may be offered the serum screening now (as well as an amniocentesis).

Weeks 17–21

- Check out the various baby equipment that is available.
- You will have your first ultrasound 'anomaly' scan during this time.
- Start doing pelvic floor exercises if you haven't already done so.
- Buy some pregnancy clothes suitable for your workplace.
- Make a birth plan.

Weeks 22–27

- Stop doing overtime.
- Read up about labour.
- Check that your diet is nutritious and remember to keep up your exercise regime.
- Get Form MAT B1 for your employer from week 26.

Weeks 28–30

- Week 29 is the first possible start date for maternity leave.
- You should take it easy around the house – don't do any heavy chores.
- You will have more frequent antenatal appointments from now.
- Start learning relaxation techniques.

Weeks 31–33

- Prepare to hand over at work.
- Antenatal classes will start now.
- Avoid flying or any other form of long-distance travel.
- Get your baby's room ready.
- Adjust to being at home.

Weeks 34–36

- Think about when to leave work if you haven't already done so. You need to give 21 days' notice.
- Pack your bag for when you go into hospital, if that is where you are having your baby.
- Check your partner's feelings about labour to ensure he is involved.

Weeks 37–40

- You will have weekly antenatal appointments from now on.
- Keep yourself mobile by doing some gentle exercise.
- Remember to pamper yourself.

planning the details

Whether your pregnancy was planned or a complete surprise, you will have to start getting ready for your baby's birth as soon as you know you are pregnant. Giving birth to a new life is a wonderful and extraordinary privilege, and it will change your own life for ever.

Pregnancy does not, and should not, go on in the background. However, most workplaces still tend to be structured by and for men, and many women feel embarrassed and uneasy about admitting to the ups and downs of pregnancy. But you and your baby must be put first, before your job. Being prepared, without panicking or trying to pretend your pregnancy isn't happening, is vital for yourself and those around you too.

Working women must consider whether their workplace is suitable for them now that they are pregnant. These areas will be looked at in more detail later on but, before you make any plans, check that you and your foetus are not in danger from any hazards that are specific to your job.

environmental pollutants These include solvents, radiation, toxic chemicals, cytotoxic drugs, cigarette smoke, carbon monoxide, mercury, lead and diseases, such as toxoplasmosis, that are carried by animals.

physical and mental stress You should consider whether the job you do is too physically demanding, either due to strenuous activity, heavy lifting or having to stand for long periods. You should also avoid excessive heat, noise, over-long hours and dangerous machinery, as all of these can add mental stress. Your company is obliged to carry out a risk assessment on your behalf and take any protective measures required, but if you think they are ill-informed or are just not interested, then consult your doctor or the Health and Safety Executive (see page 112).

unsympathetic work atmosphere If your workplace is unsympathetic to your pregnancy then you might not realize all the allowances that you are entitled to. You have a statutory right to continue working during your pregnancy, right up to the week that your baby is expected, and you are allowed reasonable time off for antenatal appointments and classes. Don't be afraid to talk to your employer about any worries – you may find their unhelpful attitude is based on a lack of understanding of your situation.

general planning

There are many things you should address at the beginning of your pregnancy.

- Work out your estimated day of delivery, or EDD (see box opposite).

- Talk to your doctor or midwife about antenatal care. You need to know how often, where, when and the duration of your hospital appointments and antenatal classes so that you can inform your workplace.
- Check your company's policy on maternity leave and benefits.
- Decide when to tell your work colleagues about your pregnancy.
- Minimize your stress levels by avoiding any unnecessary workload, excessive travelling or other work commitments that are optional.
- Consider how far into your pregnancy you want to work. It is common for women to work as long as possible, in order to have plenty of time with their baby before returning to work, but it is usually advisable to stop work by the 32nd week.
- Consider whether your present living conditions are suitable for your baby. If you do decide to move, try to do it before the last few months of your pregnancy.
- Work out a healthy eating plan, including what foods you need to cut out and how you will eat properly at work (see pages 12–13 for more details).
- Decide on a fitness programme that fits in with your working day.

ESTIMATED DATE OF DELIVERY

It is particularly important to work out your EDD as soon as possible, as you have to give your work colleagues notice of your antenatal care visits and maternity leave. You might not know the exact day that you conceived, but hopefully you will know the first day of your last menstrual period. Count 40 weeks from that, and this is your EDD. The date that you actually conceived will be around two weeks after this date, because most women tend to ovulate mid-cycle, but your doctor will calculate from the beginning of your last period, because ovulation is an inexact science so this is the most accurate method.

During the first weeks after you find out you are pregnant, you should visit your doctor or midwife to get an overview of your pregnancy and to schedule antenatal care.

health first, work second

The workplace is not always the healthiest of environments as you may have to grapple with stuffy offices, little space, time pressures and having no facilities to make your own meals as well as long hours in cramped public transport. Now that you are pregnant it is important that you put your health first and find strategies for getting round any inconveniences in your working day.

smoking

Most offices these days are no-smoking environments – the huddles of smokers in entrances and on the street attest to that. But if your office is still behind the times, you must insist that you are moved to a smoke-free area, or explain to your smoking colleagues how dangerous their habit is to your unborn baby. This really is important and should be addressed.

breaks

Do you have a proper lunch break? Many of us now work through our lunchtime, hunched over our computer with a half-eaten sandwich at our side. We all need a proper break away from our desks or working environment, but this is especially important now that you are pregnant. You need to stretch your body, get some air and eat a healthy snack. Make sure that you take an

Now is the time to put yourself and your pregnancy first, to ensure you are strong and healthy for your growing foetus.

hour's break in the middle of the day and a short break mid-morning and mid-afternoon.

food and drink

Has your workplace got a refrigerator where you can store fresh food such as fruit juice, chopped vegetables and salad? As you should be paying close attention to your diet you may find it best to prepare your own lunch, but you don't want to risk bacterial contamination. And remember to always wash your hands thoroughly before handling food.

Many companies now have water dispensers delivered, but if yours doesn't you should ensure that you bring in fresh water from home. You will need to drink plenty of fluids during the coming months.

There is no need to eliminate coffee from your diet completely during your pregnancy, but it is a stimulant, so it is wise to limit your intake of caffeine – in coffee, tea and fizzy drinks – to no more than three a day. Try keeping a supply of herbal tea, or drink hot water with a slice of lemon instead of some of those coffees.

travel

Most of us don't have many options about how we get to work, but there are some things worth considering. Do you have to stand for long periods on crowded trains or buses? If so, try to travel earlier or later to ensure that you get to sit down. Or do you spend a lot of time in traffic-congested streets biking, driving or walking to work? Carbon monoxide emissions, although only dangerous to your foetus if inhaled in large amounts, are best avoided, so consider other ways of reaching your workplace if you can.

lightening the load

You only have to look around to see women burdened with hefty briefcases, shoulder-bags and shopping. During pregnancy your body is changing, which means that you will get tired easily, and will no longer be as firm and fit as you were, so it is advisable to avoid as much extra physical strain as possible. Minimize the contents of your bag down to the bare essentials and only carry work home if you really need to. And avoid shopping on the way to or from work.

FEELING ILL AT WORK

Stuffy, cramped workplaces can result in minor ailments. If you do experience any yourself, there are alternatives to medication that you can try:

- headaches – get some fresh air, eat a light snack, drink some filtered water and hold a cold flannel to your brow. If possible lie down for half an hour.
- coughs – take some honey and a jar of fresh-squeezed lemon juice to work. Make up a mug with honey, lemon and hot water, then keep it by you to sip whenever you feel like coughing.
- muscular aches and pains – keep the affected area moving if it is stiff, and ask a colleague to massage it gently. If it is inflamed then hold a packet of frozen peas (you can take them to work in a cold bag) on the spot for two minutes on, two minutes off.

financial planning

Babies cost money, and lots of it. The first one is especially expensive as equipment for its care has to be bought from scratch. It is estimated that the overall cost of raising a child from birth to 18 is around £100,000, which sounds horrifying, but thankfully that figure is spread over a long period.

As a working mother you will also lose a percentage of your salary while you are on maternity leave. If you take the minimum time off (18 weeks) this will be approximately a third of your salary, but if you take additional maternity leave, this could rise to almost half. This deficit unfortunately comes at a time when you have the initial outlay of baby equipment to consider (see pages 88–89 for a discussion of maternity leave).

Some people also have the worry of being in a house that was fine for them as a couple, but will be too small for a family. If you are thinking of returning to work, childcare, which will be discussed later (see pages 134-37), is a major financial consideration.

working out your finances

Discuss with your partner early on how you are going to manage your finances after your baby is born so that you don't have worries at a later stage. Find out the level of benefits you can expect from your employer and work out the shortfall in your joint incomes.

Put aside, if possible, money for baby essentials, decide what level of childcare you will be able to afford and think about what luxuries, if any, you might have to forego. You may be able to ask for financial support from your immediate family if necessary. Don't rush into financial commitments, such as buying a bigger home, without considering your future employment first. For instance, you don't want to find that you are travelling long distances with the responsibility of a new baby at home. It might be better to wait until you have decided whether and when you are going back to work, and if the same job still suits you, before you move house.

mortgages

If you decide you do need a larger home, or you are concerned about the drop in income when you are on maternity leave affecting your existing mortgage payments, it is worth looking at different options. Fixed rate mortgages give you the ability to plan ahead with the exact knowledge of your monthly outgoings, but you might also consider a variable rate mortgage, which offers breaks of up to six months in which your monthly payments are suspended. This could cover the period of your maternity leave. These benefits obviously aren't free, but could be helpful if you are starting a family and your income is uncertain.

Moving house is a stressful event, so if you are thinking of doing so, try to avoid the last months of pregnancy if at all possible. You may think that where you live is too small, but it will probably do for the first few months of your baby's life.

equipment

How much can a small baby need? The answer is vast amounts, seemingly out of all proportion to the size of the recipient. It is natural to want your new baby to have only the best, and your instincts will probably tell you to rush out and buy the trendiest and most expensive buggy, cot and high chair. It is tempting, especially if you are working, to take a lunch hour and blitz the baby store without doing much research, buying everything that you will need in one go. However, it is wise to wait until the end of the first three months before buying anything, so that the risk of miscarriage has lessened.

You may not actually need to buy everything new. Talk to friends, relatives or colleagues at work who have just had babies and see what equipment they have, what they bought and never used, and what has been essential. Most babies grow very quickly in the first six months, so it is sensible to borrow the smallest size baby clothes from friends rather than spending money on garments your baby might only wear for a week.

if you're on your own

Even if you have chosen to be a single mother, it can be very daunting to face the momentous and life-altering events of pregnancy and birth when you are on your own. Not only is it unlikely that you will have the luxury of choosing whether you work or not, but there is an implied criticism in society about single parenthood that can make you feel guilty and worry that you are letting your baby down. However, don't waste time on guilt that is totally unnecessary – concentrate instead on supporting you and your child's future financially and emotionally. This means that you will need to line up a network of support from family and friends and find good childcare before the birth.

Even if you are planning to continue working after the birth, it's particularly important to check out any special benefits that you might be entitled to. There are single parent organizations that can help you with this and you should contact them as soon as possible (see page 113). If the baby's father is still in contact with you, work out what his financial contribution is going to be. The Child Support Agency can sometimes help if there are problems keeping in touch.

If you are on your own you will need to find a birth partner. Ask a close friend or relative, but make sure you choose someone with whom you feel comfortable and who will be reliable and strong during the birth.

As a single working mother, you need reliable back-up childcare for when the main carer isn't available. This can be a neighbour or relative, as long as he or she lives near enough to take over in an emergency to avoid you being unreliable for work.

clinic services

Antenatal care is mostly provided by your midwife or midwifery team. Some of the care may also be provided by your GP, and some by the obstetric team (the hospital-based group of doctors, midwives and nurses who specialize in pregnancy). You are also entitled to ask for your pregnancy care to be provided by a different GP from the one with whom you are registered if you want to.

If you do decide that you would prefer to have another doctor during your pregnancy, you can still stay registered to your original GP. You may have come to this decision because you feel that your current GP may not be the right person for your pregnancy care, or the surgery does not provide the service (some smaller surgeries do not).

Increasingly, obstetricians are actually concentrating on abnormal or at-risk pregnancies. So an increasing number of pregnant women are not seen at any stage by an obstetrician, with no loss of quality of care. Midwives are, after all, the experts in the management of normal pregnancies.

You may attend hospital for some specialized tests, such as an ultrasound scan, or if problems or potential problems are identified in the course of your pregnancy. Otherwise your care will be provided by midwives in your doctor's surgery, or at home. Both the hospital and your doctor's surgery will be near to where you live, and this might mean they are quite a distance from your place of work. You must allow for travelling time and long waits when informing your work of your clinic visits. It is sensible to take the whole morning or afternoon off so that you aren't worried by unforeseen delays.

how often?

Surprisingly, there is no general agreement on how often you should be seen by either your doctor or your midwife during your pregnancy. There is a feeling that the number of visits has, for some time, been more than really necessary, and many areas are now reducing the amount. A common pattern is for two visits in the first 24 weeks or so, then monthly until 32 weeks, fortnightly until 36 weeks and then weekly till the birth. Do not be alarmed if you are scheduled for fewer visits than you expected, these reductions are based on good research. Your first visit (the booking visit) will be the longest. Your full medical history will be taken, as well as details of your family's medical problems, and there will be discussion about the way your pregnancy will be managed. In addition you will be told about the tests you may be offered during pregnancy (see routine blood tests, pages 30–31). They will also carry out a physical examination, feeling your stomach to see if the womb can be felt (it usually cannot be felt before 12 weeks), checking your breasts and possibly giving an internal examination to assess the progress of the pregnancy by the size and shape of the womb. You will also have a blood and urine sample taken, be weighed and measured and your blood pressure checked. Using a hand-held instrument, the midwife will listen for the sound of your baby's heartbeat (audible at 14 weeks). The magnified beat sounds impossibly fast (160 beats per minute or more), but this is normal, and it is thrilling to hear your baby for the first time.

The timing of your booking visit will depend on the policies in your local maternity unit. You should be given plenty of warning about this appointment, but do ask to change it if it is inconvenient. This is the most important visit of your pregnancy, and it is essential to be able to spend as much time as is needed at this first visit.

At each subsequent appointment the midwife or doctor will check your blood pressure, take a urine sample and sometimes a blood sample. They will check your baby's heartbeat and conduct an abdominal palpation, where they feel for the height of the uterus and, later, for the way the baby is lying. They may look at your ankles to make sure you aren't retaining too much fluid.

antenatal classes

Your clinic, whether in a hospital or doctor's surgery, may also offer antenatal and parentcraft classes for first-time parents, usually starting around 30–31 weeks. These are optional, and you may feel you can't take any more time off work to attend them, but this is a mistake. As a working woman you will not have the opportunity to discuss your pregnancy much, so these classes are invaluable. They allow you to find out about labour and voice concerns that you or your partner might have. It is also extremely helpful to be with others who are going through the same experience.

Most antenatal classes usually last between one and a half to two hours for a minimum of six sessions. They all follow a similar format and cover the same subject matter. You will be taught relaxation and breathing techniques for labour, and be offered a range of information from how to recognize the onset of labour, when to go to the hospital, pain relief in childbirth and how to care for your baby as well as what to expect emotionally and physically as a new parent. Try to take your partner with you to these classes so that he can provide as much support as possible for you as well as learn about his part in the whole experience. Some classes teach toning and strengthening exercises or recommend a separate class. Some hospital-run classes will arrange visits to maternity wards during your pregnancy.

Your employer is obliged by law to give you reasonable time off work, with pay at your normal rate, for antenatal and parentcraft classes (see pages 88–91 for further details).

supplements and drugs

Whether or not to take vitamin and mineral supplements continues to be a hotly debated point with health professionals. However, unless you are eating a very poor, unbalanced diet, there should be no need for supplements during your pregnancy, with the exception of folic acid and occasionally iron. And it is also important that you stay away from any sort of medication – even some herbal remedies can put your baby at risk.

You should aim to get your daily requirement of vitamins and minerals from a healthy, balanced diet, even if this takes a bit of ingenuity at work. We are lucky these days, because our increasingly health-conscious society means that there is a lot of healthy takeaway food such as baked potatoes, fresh soups, salads and wholegrain sandwiches.

folic acid

Because adequate levels of folic acid in your body encourage the correct development of your baby's spine, spinal cord and brain (and this occurs in the early weeks of pregnancy), you should take a supplement of 400 micrograms of folic acid per day as soon as you know you are pregnant until the 12th week of your pregnancy. If you are planning a pregnancy, it is best to start taking this supplementation three months before you start trying to conceive. You can obtain folic acid from your diet by eating broccoli, spinach, peas, leafy green vegetables, bananas, pulses and some cereal and bread available in supermarkets that has been fortified with folic acid. A folic acid deficiency can result in neural tube defects such as spina bifida, cleft palate and anencephaly (see page 36). But now that folic acid supplements are routinely taken in early pregnancy, these defects are very much rarer than they were – in fact they are now very rare indeed.

iron

Iron is an essential part of haemoglobin, the molecule within the red blood cell that carries oxygen from the lungs to the rest of the body. Because a baby uses up much of a mother's iron reserves, some women become deficient in iron, and may become anaemic. In the developed world, severe anaemia is rare, but some pregnant women are prescribed iron supplements to prevent a major drop in haemoglobin levels. However, you can also obtain iron by eating wholegrains, egg yolks, dark green leafy vegetables, molasses, red meat and dried peas and beans. Vitamin C helps in the absorption of iron, while caffeine hinders it, so avoid coffee and drink a glass of fresh orange juice instead.

Most prescription drugs should be avoided in pregnancy, but supplements like folic acid are considered essential in the first 12 weeks.

drugs during pregnancy

A baby is well protected in the womb from dangers, however you should always be aware of the fact that everything you eat, drink and breathe in during your pregnancy has the potential to harm your baby. Most of us take over-the-counter medicines, such as pain killers, antibiotics, cough mixture and anti-histamines without much thought. Taken in pregnancy, these seemingly innocuous chemicals cross the placenta, enter the baby's bloodstream and can accumulate in toxic quantities, which may affect development.

Obviously you have to strike a balance between being very ill, which can also be detrimental to your growing foetus, and taking drugs that might cause harm. But it is better to avoid all unnecessary medication during pregnancy. If you are ill and feel you need medication, consult your doctor first.

Illegal drugs such as cocaine, cannabis, heroin, LSD, Ecstasy and amphetamines have all been shown to carry potentially major risks such as heart defects, blood diseases, chromosomal damage, miscarriage and addiction in which the baby suffers withdrawal symptoms at birth. These drugs must on no account be used when you are pregnant.

Creams and ointments used during pregnancy can be as dangerous as a drug taken internally, as the substance can be passed to your baby by absorption through the skin. Normal body lotions are fine, but avoid creams that contain any active ingredient. If in doubt, consult your doctor before using something.

herbal remedies

We all like to think that herbal remedies are perfectly safe, but the chemicals that are used synthetically in conventional medicine have often been derived from plant sources. There are many excellent herbal remedies for use in pregnancy, but also many that are dangerous, so don't take any remedy, either herbal or conventional, before first checking whether it is considered safe. If you are in doubt, then avoid it completely.

What will I feel like? When will the baby show? Will I be well enough to work? When should I tell my employer? Will I get over-emotional and irrational and, if so, will this affect my job? What should I wear for work? Should I exercise and, if so, when can I fit it in? These are some of the questions that a first-time working mother-to-be might ask. This week-by-week section provides you with all the answers.

Being pregnant is a strange and exciting phenomenon and it is very important that you are able to enjoy this special time, and that you view it as a normal progression in your life and work. You can easily combine pregnancy with your daily routine and take the steps that are vital to ensure the health of yourself and your baby in the coming months. As a working woman you will have to plan more rigorously than a woman who has her own schedule, so the following section is designed to make this as easy as possible, to ensure you take the changes in your stride.

The different considerations you will need to face through the weeks leading up to your baby's birth will all be discussed in detail here: the health and development of your baby; your own emotional and physical health, including diet and exercise; the medical care you can expect, including birth plans; and, most importantly, how you can best fit each of these areas into your working schedule. Remember that every woman's pregnancy is different. Some sail through with no problems at all, while some experience discomfort. This section is not meant to be taken as gospel, it is just a guide. If heartburn is mentioned, for instance, it doesn't necessarily mean that you will suffer from it. Take a general view and use the information provided here to plan and make decisions to ensure you can embrace a healthy, straightforward pregnancy, all the while looking forward to the birth of your baby.

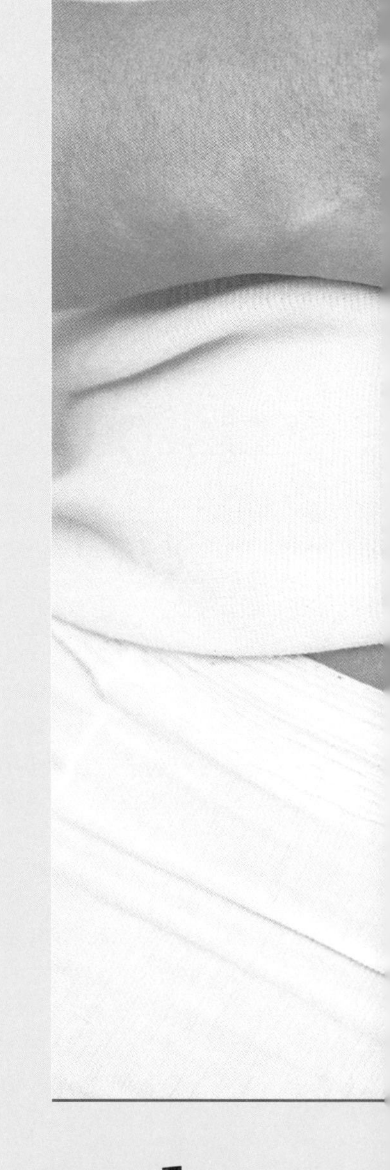

week-by-week guide

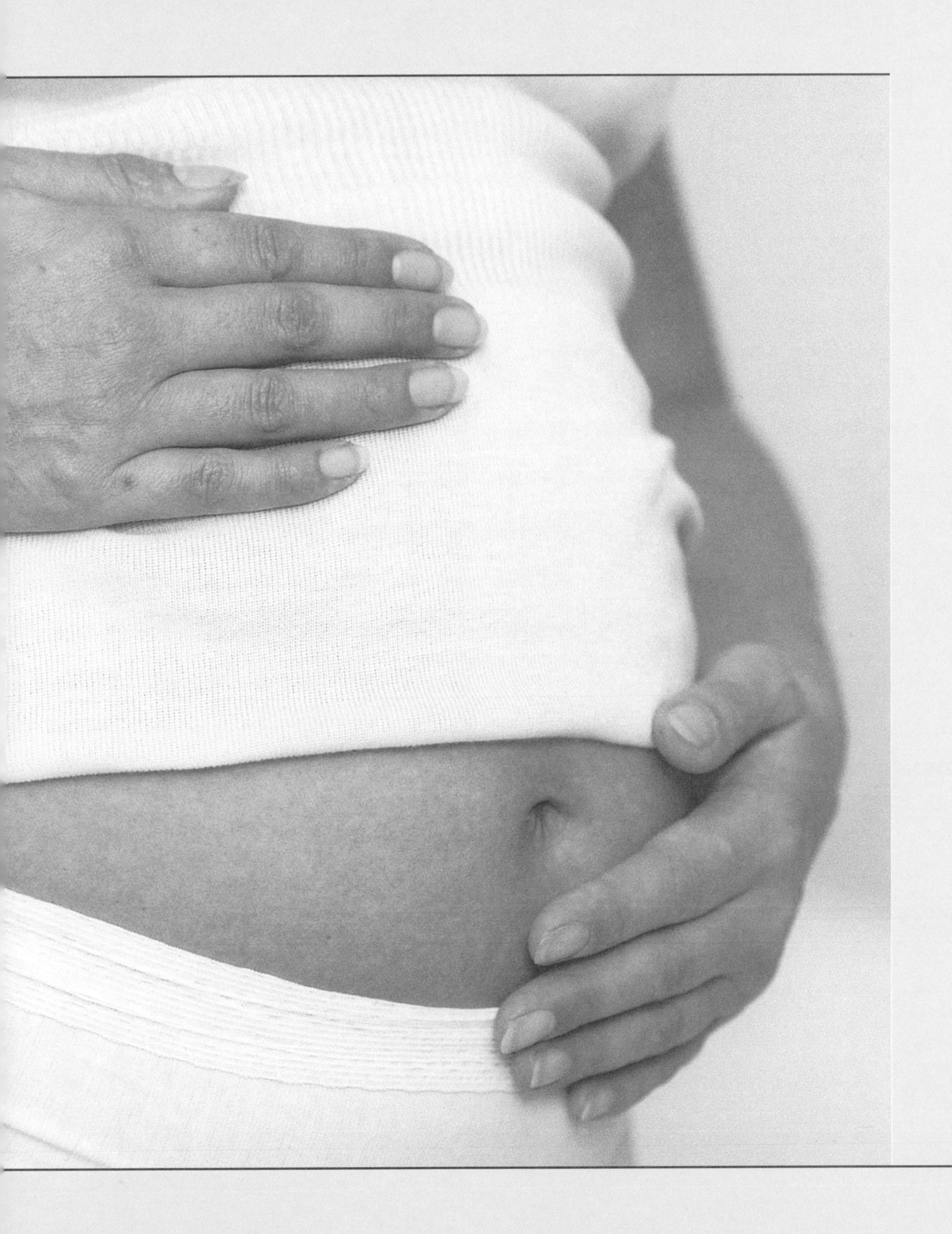

weeks 1–7

Many women describe the first few weeks of pregnancy as unreal. The thought that there is another life stirring inside them seems unbelievable. This euphoric state is often also accompanied by physical changes beyond the missed period, such as sensitive breasts, nausea, an enhanced sense of smell or taste, passing urine more frequently and unusual tiredness. These things are all normal and it is important to realize that you will feel different from now on.

weeks	lifestyle changes	medical care	diet
1–7	Now is the time to give up smoking. Cigarettes restrict the transfer of oxygen to your baby and there is also a greater risk of miscarriage and lower birth weight.	During these early weeks the foetus is particularly at risk from drugs. This is when your baby's major organ systems are being formed, and some drugs cause malformations in the foetus. If you are on any medication, tell your doctor as soon as you suspect you are pregnant. Avoid over-the-counter drugs (see page 19) and illegal substances such as cannabis, Ecstasy, cocaine or heroin.	Your feelings about food may alter a lot in the first weeks (such as losing appetite or changing tastes). But you must eat regularly and nutritiously.
	Alcohol is also best avoided as it passes through the placenta to the baby and can cause foetal abnormalities, low birth weight and increased risk of miscarriage.		All pregnant women should drink ½ litre (1 pint) of milk a day as your baby's bones and teeth begin to form early in pregnancy and calcium is vital for developing them.
	You should check out your company's maternity policy now and find out what they offer beyond the statutory maternity pay.	Visit your doctor or midwife as soon as you suspect you are pregnant.	Remember to take your folic acid supplement as it is vital for your baby's development (see page 18 for details).

your baby

Your pregnancy is dated from the day you began your last period. Because you become pregnant roughly two weeks after this date, the true age of the foetus is two weeks less than this. This means, for instance, that when you are seven weeks pregnant, your foetus is five weeks old. It measures up to 1.5cm (½in), (the crown-rump measurement from its head to its tail), which is about the size of a large pea, and it will look as if it is mostly head. Its chest and tummy are distinct bulges.

At this very early stage of your pregnancy there is a simple tube inside your foetus that will gradually develop into your baby's heart.

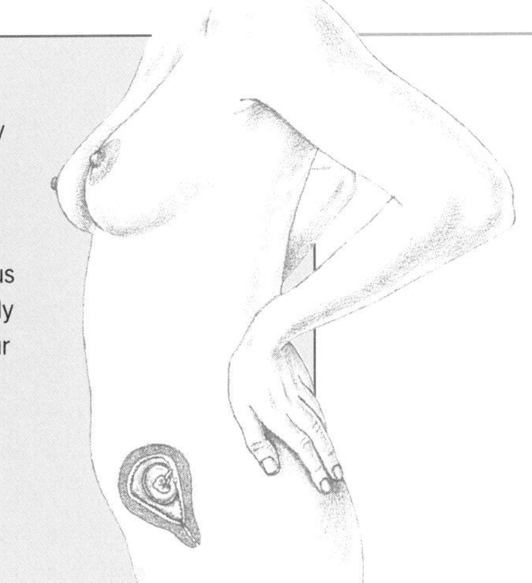

emotions

By the seventh week of pregnancy, the placenta will have begun to take over production of hormones such as oestrogen and progesterone, which help develop and maintain your pregnancy. Hormonal changes affect emotions so you might swing between high excitement, disbelief and nervousness at the responsibility you now have for the baby you are carrying.

You might find it hard to concentrate on your work and be anxious about the implications to your career. This is all normal and your emotions will settle down by around week 12.

exercise

There is no evidence that vigorous exercise can cause damage to a pregnancy, but it seems sensible to avoid dangerous sports during pregnancy, and to avoid any excessive physical straining.

You will probably find, even at this early stage, that you tire more quickly than you used to, and may also feel faint, so you will need to amend any regular exercise programme to take this into account.

clothing

You won't look pregnant yet, but you might already feel generally heavier and could have gained around two pounds (less than one kilo). This won't mean that you have to wear a larger size in clothes yet, but you probably won't feel comfortable with anything tight round your waist. Therefore, you should opt for the things that you already have in your wardrobe that are less restrictive. This is especially necessary during a long day at work.

weeks

1–7

miscarriage

Most foetal problems can be highlighted by ultrasound scans and other tests, but some will have immediate effects, including miscarriage. About 15 per cent of recognized pregnancies miscarry, but the overall loss of conceptions (fertilized eggs) may be as high as 50 per cent, many of which are not recognized as miscarriages by mothers because they were not aware that they were pregnant. After the 13th week of pregnancy the chances of miscarriage are reduced.

Ultrasound scans are used to monitor your baby's progress, and can successfully highlight problems and confirm your due date.

Most miscarriages are thought to be caused by a fundamental defect in the foetus, and it is appropriate that the pregnancy miscarries. Some miscarriages will be due to illness or to infections such as listeriosis, toxoplasmosis and others (see opposite). Often there is no obvious explanation.

If you experience heavy bleeding and pass blood clots in association with cramps similar to, but worse than, menstrual cramps, you may be at high risk of losing the pregnancy. Unfortunately there is no medical intervention that can affect the outcome at this point. Many women have slight blood loss in the early weeks of pregnancy without things progressing to a miscarriage, but any loss of

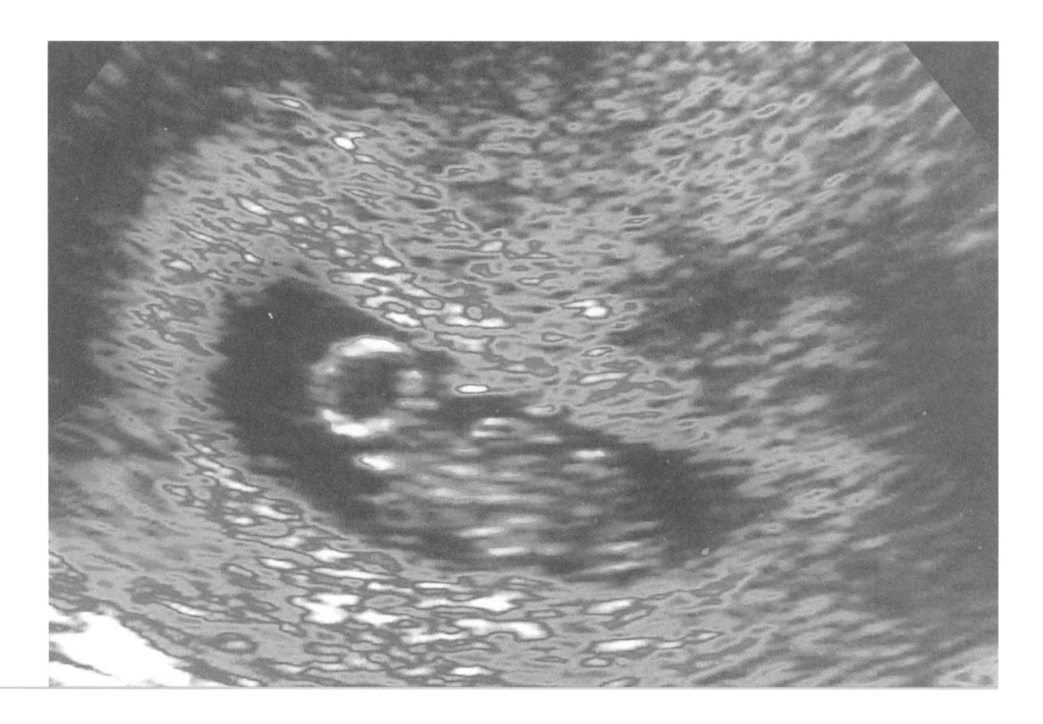

blood should be reported immediately to your midwife or doctor. If you do experience blood loss in early pregnancy, you should probably slow down a bit. It is up to you whether you stop work or not and it also depends, to a certain extent, on the type of work you do. There is no evidence that it makes any difference to the outcome, but you may feel a lot better generally if you take it easy.

Coming to terms with a miscarriage can be very hard. Feelings of bereavement and anger, but especially worry that there is something wrong with you or that you are somehow to blame, are common. Your work environment can be especially trying at a time like this. You might not know the best way to tell your colleagues about your miscarriage. If this is worrying you, talk to a sympathetic work mate, or your employer, and ask them to tell the others. Decide whether or not you want to discuss it and let them know. Most people find that talking helps, but you might feel the workplace is not the right environment for this. Give yourself time to recover, take a few days off and get plenty of rest and pampering before plunging back into work.

rubella

Rubella (German measles), if contracted in the first few weeks of pregnancy, can have very serious effects on your baby. Most women in the West will have been immunized in childhood, and that immunity will be effective as an adult. However, it is sensible to check your immunity prior to getting pregnant if you work with children or travel abroad a lot in your job, as these might expose you to the condition. The test is a simple blood test, which can be easily arranged by your doctor.

food-borne infection

If you are eating takeaway food while at work, make sure it is as fresh as possible or has been stored at the right temperature. The two most worrying food-borne infections are listeriosis and toxoplasmosis, but neither is common, although both can cause miscarriage and foetal damage. Avoid unpasteurized soft cheese such as dolcelatte, camembert and brie, undercooked chicken, pork and lamb, and pâtés and raw meats, all of which are known to carry risks of contamination. There are other infections that can be contracted from undercooked meats and eggs, such as e-coli and salmonella. Chlamydia psittaci (not to be confused with the sexually transmitted chlamydia trachomatis), on the other hand, can be caught from infected birds and sheep. (See the 'working safely' section on pages 82-83, for further details about the symptoms of these diseases, where they are a specific hazard of particular jobs.)

You should always be vigilant about the hygiene measures that you take. If you decide to take your own food into your workplace, then you should make sure that you store it at a suitably low temperature, either in a refrigerator or a cool bag. And always wash your hands well and frequently, especially just before handling food.

understanding antenatal notes

Unlike in the past, we now have access to our antenatal notes. But many of the terms will be incomprehensible to anyone without medical training, and they can therefore seem alarming. Here, some of the most common terms are explained but if you have any worries about what a particular reading indicates, don't hesitate to ask your midwife for a fuller explanation.

Many doctors don't involve the patient enough because of time restrictions or because they feel the woman either doesn't want to know or won't understand. It's your baby and your choice as to how much information you have. If you are worried you won't be given a chance to ask questions, or will be too nervous, write a list before you go to an antenatal appointment, or take someone with you who will ask for you. You may well find you are highly emotional and anxious if faced with complex information hurled at you in a hurry, and having someone else to take it in can be very reassuring.

ABBREVIATIONS EXPLAINED

- **bp** This is your blood pressure reading. It can vary, and one reading cannot be taken as a concrete indication of a problem. You might have been hurrying and anxious, it might be very hot or you might have had too much caffeine. If it is high, over 140/90, it will be taken again later. Only if it reads consistently high will they consider taking any action such as putting you on medication to bring it down, as high blood pressure is more damaging to a foetus than properly prescribed medicine.
- **cx** This is the abbreviation for your cervix, the neck of the uterus which, when it begins to soften, heralds the start of labour.
- **edd** Estimated date of delivery.
- **eng** This indicates that the head is engaged, which is when the widest part of your baby's head drops down into your pelvis ready for labour. This can happen as early as six weeks before labour commences, but it can vary.
- **fe** Explains that iron has been prescribed.
- **fh** This means foetal heart; your baby's heart rate and audibility is noted from early on.
- **fmf** Means that foetal movements were felt.
- **hb/hgb** This refers to haemoglobin, which is the measure used to check for anaemia. A good level would be around 12gm, while anything below 10gm might result in you being prescribed iron supplements.
- **height of fundus: h o f** The fundus is the top of the uterus, which is pushed upwards, approximately 1cm (0.39in) a week during pregnancy, and this is a rough indication of your baby's growth.
- **h/t** Means hypertension (high blood pressure). Your doctor will monitor this.

- **lmp** This is the first day of your last menstrual period.
- **msu** Stands for midstream urine sample.
- **oed** This is the abbreviation for oedema, which means that you are experiencing swelling due to fluid retention, usually in the extremities. Excessive or sudden oedema can be an indication of problems with the pregnancy. However, most women will notice some fluid retention during pregnancy without experiencing oedema.
- **para 0** This means that you have not had any previous births. 'para 1', etc, will indicate number of previous births.
- **pp** The presenting part is the lowest part of your baby when he is lying in the womb, so is the part that will present at the cervix first. This could be followed by 'Vx' (vertex), 'ceph' (cephalic – the head is first), 'Br' (breech – the head is up not down and the bottom is first) or 'Tr' (transverse – your baby is lying across you). By the end of your pregnancy, these terms get more technical, and indicate in greater detail the position of your baby.
- **t** This means your baby is ready to be born, but is not a guarantee of imminent delivery!
- **urine test** This might say NAD under it, which means 'no abnormality detected', or 'nil'. 'Prot' means that protein has been detected in your urine. This could be a sign of pre-eclampsia, but many women have occasional traces of protein, and it is not, by itself, a cause for alarm.
- **ve** This means that you had a vaginal examination during the appointment.

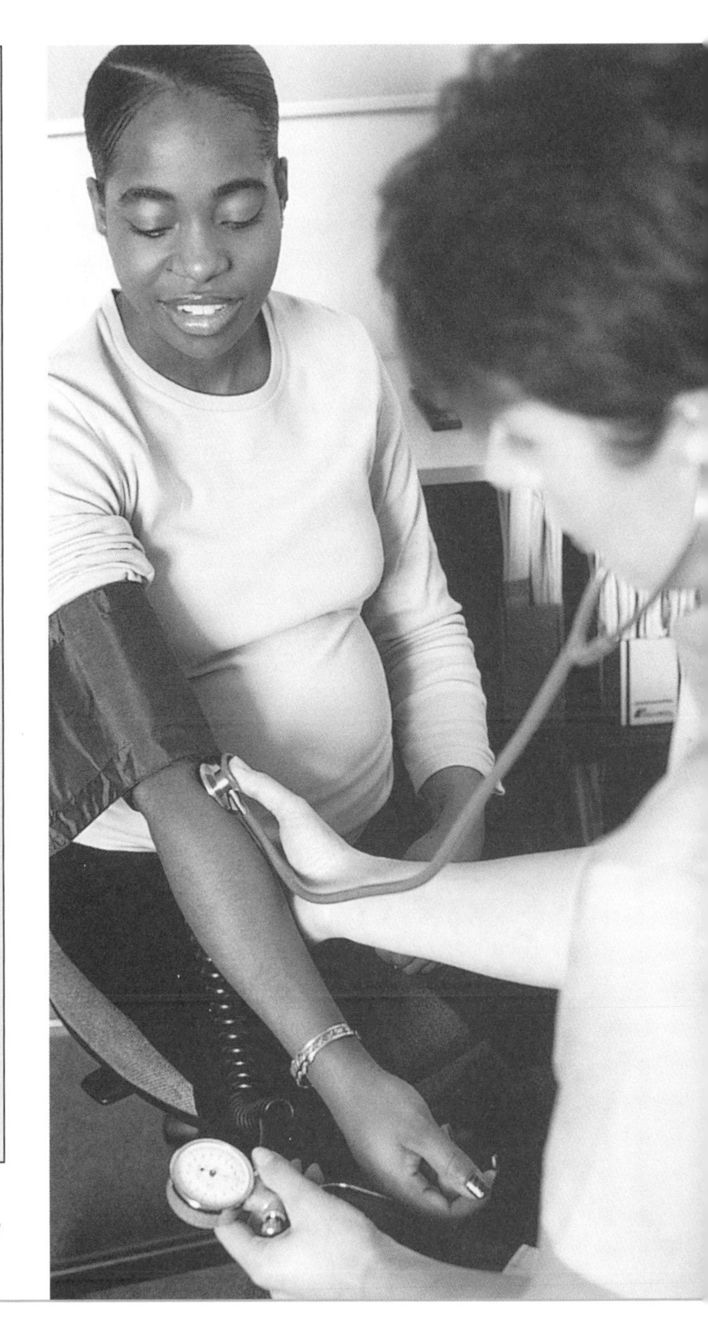

Thorough testing at your appointments should ensure a healthy, trouble-free pregnancy.

weeks 8–12

Have you told your employer that you are pregnant yet? There is no legal requirement to do so until 21 days before you start your maternity leave in order to secure your maternity rights, but it is advisable to let them know earlier because of your antenatal appointments, for legal protection against dismissal and unfair treatment on the grounds of pregnancy and as a courtesy of giving management enough time to find a suitable replacement.

weeks	lifestyle changes	medical care	diet
8–12	Morning sickness can be a problem from around the 6th week of pregnancy until the 16th, and it often peaks in the 9th week. Caused primarily by a rise in the levels of hormones linked to pregnancy, it is usually at its worst in the mornings when you haven't eaten for a while, but can occur at other times. It is often triggered by strong smells or tastes. If you are suffering from nausea, make sure you eat small amounts regularly, especially first thing in the morning, when a plain biscuit and glass of milk or water can help stave off the sickness.	Around the 12th week will be the time that you have your first antenatal booking appointment. Make sure you allow plenty of time for this visit, as it is the longest (see page 17 for details of what happens at this and the subsequent antenatal appointments, too). You will be told about the various different tests that are available for detecting foetal abnormalities at your first appointment. The nuchal translucency scan and chorionic villus sampling tests are carried out around this time (see pages 30–31).	Having the right food to hand can be a problem for the working woman unless you take a supply of food with you to your workplace. Fill a lunchbox with snacks, such as chopped vegetables, hard-boiled eggs, cubes of cheese and fruit and crackers, and make sure you have a supply of filtered water and fruit juice handy. If the office has no facilities for keeping things cold, take a small insulated bag to work. If you are suffering from morning sickness while at work, take glucose sweets with you as well as high-fibre carbohydrate snacks, such as oat cakes or bananas.

your baby

Your baby is growing rapidly and is approximately 6.5cm (2½in) by the 12th week. The sex organs are now definably male or female and the nervous system can send messages to the muscles allowing the baby to make her first movements, such as curling her toes. Your blood will be tested for Rhesus blood group around week 12. If your blood is Rhesus negative and the baby's father's is Rhesus positive, it is possible that your baby's will be Rhesus positive, and you may need protective injections.

If Rhesus positive blood cells escape into the maternal blood, they react to form Rhesus antibodies. See page 31 for details.

Key
+ Rhesus positive blood
- Rhesus negative blood
⊕ Rhesus antibodies

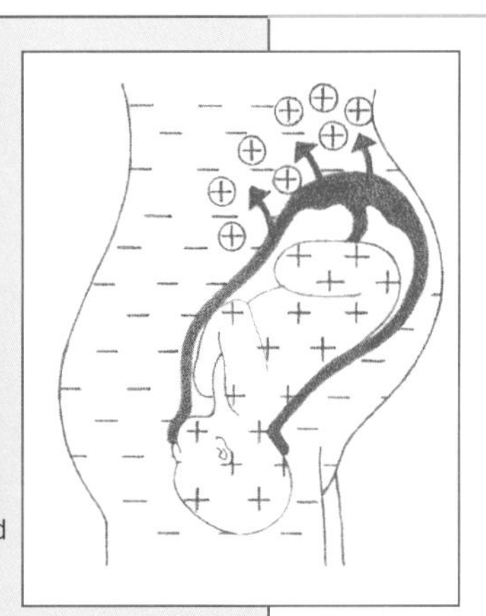

emotions

Some women are overcome by sudden waves of tiredness in the early weeks. This is said to be due to the increased levels of the hormone progesterone, but emotional and physical changes must also take some responsibility. You may be excited and not sleeping properly, or you may be suffering from morning sickness, which is also tiring.

Reduce social engagements for a while and get plenty of sleep, or take a nap when you get home from work. If you get too tired you will be over-emotional and irritable, and your relationships with your colleagues and partner will suffer.

exercise

Regular, gentle exercise during pregnancy can help backache, breathlessness, cramp and constipation. Your figure returns to normal more quickly after the birth too.

Be realistic when choosing what type of exercise to do. There are exercise and yoga classes for pregnant women but take into account your previous exercise levels. Your hormones circulating in your blood will cause your ligaments to soften, which means you must take care not to put them under any strain. Make sure that any exercises you do have been designed for pregnancy.

clothing

This is the time to buy a new bra. Your breasts will swell quite considerably in the first three months and you will need a maternity bra that offers the proper support, with wide straps and a comfortable band that won't ride up or dig in. It is best to be measured and fitted to find the right size. Don't buy too many bras at this stage, as you might need a larger size in the months to come.

In addition to this, if you are used to wearing a tight-fitting blouse or suit to work, or you have to wear a uniform, you will need to invest in a larger size, or resort to a looser style of dress.

testing methods

The vast majority of babies will be born healthy but, unfortunately, some will not. Major advances have been made in recent years in the recognition of babies with congenital (present at birth) abnormality while they are still in the womb. This has enabled couples either to be forewarned about abnormality, and to plan for it, or to discuss termination of the affected pregnancy.

Many abnormalities will be discovered at the ultrasound 'anomaly' scan (see page 40), but many others cannot be detected by ultrasound scan. The most important group of abnormalities in this category is the group of chromosomal anomalies, of which Down's syndrome is the commonest. Several options are now available for those couples who want to try to determine whether their baby is affected. The simplest is to be guided by your age: for all maternal ages it is possible to quote the 'odds' – the older you are, the more likely the baby is to be affected. However, it is now possible to provide couples with odds based on tests that look more specifically at their own individual pregnancy.

nuchal translucency scan This is done at around 11 weeks. It is a test that has no risk to your baby other than the (very small) theoretical risk of ultrasound. The nuchal fold, at the back of the baby's neck, is measured, and this is analysed by computer software. The test cannot diagnose a chromosomal defect, but it will give you the odds of one occurring, eg 1 in 205, 1 in 3230, based on the fold's thickness and your age. Using this test it is estimated that 60–70 per cent of Down's syndrome babies can be detected prenatally. At present not many maternity services provide this test, but it is widely available privately. The other way to find out whether your baby might be affected is to have a serum screening test (see page 36). The test is without risk to your baby and many, but not all, maternity services provide this test. Probably 60 per cent of Down's syndrome babies will be picked up by this test. If the test indicated that you had a high risk of your baby being affected, you might then choose to have a further test to indicate whether your baby definitely was or was not affected. There are two such further tests: chorionic villus biopsy and amniocentesis.

chorionic villus biopsy For this a tiny sample of the placental tissue is taken, either by means of a vaginal approach or through the abdominal wall. It is performed at about the 9th–11th week, allowing for a diagnosis to be made early on, which has advantages if a termination may be considered. However, it carries a 2 per cent risk of causing the pregnancy to miscarry, and so it is not performed unless there are good reasons for doing so. This test is much less frequently used than amniocentesis is (see page 36).

routine blood tests

Most routine blood tests are taken at the first antenatal appointment but some are then repeated later on. The most common include:

blood group You must know whether you are Rhesus group negative or positive. If the baby's father is Rhesus positive, it is possible that your baby will be Rhesus positive. In this case, Rhesus negative mothers may develop antibodies to their baby's blood. These antibodies may damage the developing baby's blood in subsequent pregnancies. Fortunately you can be given protective Anti-D antibodies if needed, to protect against this occurring. Increasingly maternity services are routinely giving Rhesus negative mothers Anti-D injections during their first pregnancies. Ask your midwife if this is the local policy.

haemoglobin This test is to find out whether you are anaemic. The test is measured in grams per decilitre, and a level of more than 10 is satisfactory. If you have less than that you may need to take iron supplements. This test will then be repeated at least once.

rubella immunity This is tested to ensure your childhood immunization is still effective.

hepatitis B You will be tested to see if you have ever had Hepatitis B. If you have had it, you may be infectious to your baby. If so, your baby can be given protective treatment at birth. It is very rare to test positive to this.

HIV (human immunodeficiency virus) Pregnant women are strongly encouraged to be tested for HIV. Action can be taken to substantially reduce the risk of transmission to the baby.

syphilis Syphilis, which has been routinely tested for for decades, can cause foetal damage but is easily treatable with antibiotics. Again, it is also very rare.

urine sample

Each time you attend an appointment at the antenatal clinic you will be asked to take a urine sample with you in a sterilized pot that will be provided. It is best to do the sample at home, before you go to work on the day of your appointment. Your urine will then be tested for sugar. High sugar levels could indicate 'gestational' diabetes, a form that goes away after the pregnancy is over, but could affect the baby if it is not treated by diet and careful monitoring. Without this, a baby can be exposed to excessive sugar supplied through the placenta and can become very large, making labour difficult and a caesarean section likely. There is also a risk of heart and respiratory problems in the baby.

Your urine is also tested for protein. If this is present it could be a sign of an infection or, more importantly, of a potentially serious condition called pre-eclampsia, or pre-eclamptic toxaemia. This can cause the placenta to fail, and your baby to be born prematurely and is accompanied by high blood pressure and fluid retention. It is important to recognize this condition early. The cause is not fully understood, but women at a higher risk include those over 35, those who are pregnant for the first time, women with gestational diabetes and those who are having a multiple pregnancy.

stress relief

Pregnancy can be a very stressful time, especially if you are working. Many women sail through without any problems at all, but there are others who find balancing their job with the upheaval of their changing body and emotions, not to mention the responsibility of another human life, quite daunting.

It is easy to think that you somehow must still be able to do everything: to continue to work with the speed and dedication you always have done, to look your best, pursue a hectic social life, keep the house clean and give dinner parties etc. There are some women who can do all this, but for the majority it is much better to opt for a more realistic schedule during your pregnancy and early motherhood. In the bigger scheme of things, pregnancy does not last for long, and you should aim for the minimum of unnecessary stress while it does.

partner support

Many people see pregnancy as purely the domain of women. But your partner is 50 per cent responsible for the baby you are now carrying, and you must include him in every aspect right from the start. You may already share the domestic chores, but if you don't, start now. Ask him to do all the heavy work, such as carrying the shopping home.

work stress

Your job may be inherently stressful, you can't help that, but you can help the attitude you take towards it. During your pregnancy you must be firm and cut out extra-curricular activities, overtime, optional job training and too much social entertaining and travelling. If you begin to realize that you are exhausted, take steps to slow down. If you ignore the signs it could result in serious problems for you and your baby in the future.

planning

'Be prepared' is the old Boy Scout motto, and you will be more relaxed about your pregnancy if you learn more about what happens. Read up about both pregnancy and labour so that you know what to expect. Plan the weeks ahead carefully with regard to maternity leave, antenatal care, the birth plan (see page 40) and shopping for your baby as well as your job handover.

relaxation

Relaxation comes in lots of different forms – from a warm bath to a sophisticated breathing technique – but you will need to make sure that you have good chunks of free time in order to enjoy any of them. If you arrive home from work and immediately start to hoover, rush out to some party or make hundreds of phone calls, you won't have any proper relaxation time. It isn't easy finding time for yourself when you are working hard, but it really is important that you do so while you are pregnant.

Try incorporating little things in your day in order to pamper yourself, as this is the time to put yourself first. For example, buy yourself a luxurious bath oil or get some dried herbs with a soothing scent such as lavender to put on your desk. You may find it is comforting to keep a soft shawl in your desk drawer to wrap around you during your breaks. Alternatively, book an aromatherapy massage for your lunch hour. Be sure that only oils safe during pregnancy are used.

You should also make time each day for a gentle exercise regime, as this will benefit both you and the baby. You must be prepared to cancel social engagements if you are feeling tired too.

stay healthy

You will be carrying lots of extra baby weight in the months ahead, which will be tiring in itself, but try to avoid putting on unnecessary pounds by eating too much of the wrong sort of food. Eating lots of sugary, fatty foods will make you feel tired and run down. You will need more calories than usual for the baby's development, but make sure that they come from wholefoods, fruit and vegetables, with the odd treat thrown in, rather than the other way around.

If you think you will find this difficult, then try treating yourself to inviting but healthy food – buy organic juice to drink during your working day and some delicious fruits to nibble on, such as strawberries, passion fruit and peaches. If you decide you don't feel up to cooking, ask your partner to do it instead.

Reduce the stress around you by knowing when to ask for help, staying healthy and learning how to relax.

weeks 13–16

Now you are over the first three months of pregnancy the threat of miscarriage is very small. You will also be looking pregnant by the end of week 16. This means that if you haven't told your work colleagues they will probably begin to guess. Getting used to the new status of being a pregnant woman can be quite strange and you will find that your thoughts constantly divert to the new life inside you. You should be thinking about your antenatal care and when you may want to start your maternity leave.

weeks	lifestyle changes	medical care	diet
13–16	A pregnancy at work can be unsettling for those around you. There is the uncertainty of whether you will return after the baby's birth and can also be a fear that you will pay less attention to your work now and others will have to pick up the slack. There may even be those who envy you or are thinking about competing for your job. Although most people will be happy for you, you should be aware of how your situation affects those around you. Be as decisive as you can about antenatal care and maternity leave and try to stick to your plans.	You may be offered a serum screening test to check for the risk of chromosomal abnormality. If you are an older mother (over 35) or your serum screening was abnormal, the doctor might suggest that you have an amniocentesis too. You may begin to experience some heartburn and minor digestive problems at this stage as the baby takes up more room in your abdomen and the musculature of your intestinal tract relaxes (see page 44). Make sure you eat small meals and sleep propped up with a pillow.	You will probably be feeling much hungrier than you usually do by now. This is very normal and it is actually important that you eat more than you would normally as this extra food will fuel your baby's rapid development. Therefore, don't allow yourself to get too hungry, but don't fall into the trap of snacking on junk food either. Eat small, nutritious meals regularly throughout the day; it is often easier to take your own food into work in order to be able to do this (see pages 12–13).

your baby

At 16 weeks your baby's fingers, nose and toes are fully formed, although the head is still large in comparison to the body. The baby now contains the same number of nerve cells as you do, and by the end of week 16 will measure 11.5cm (4½in). The bones are beginning to harden throughout his body. Your baby can hear your voice and your heartbeat by now, and he can even suck his thumb too!

During amniocentesis around 15ml of amniotic fluid is drawn through a fine needle and sent for laboratory analysis. An ultrasound scan is used to guide the needle.

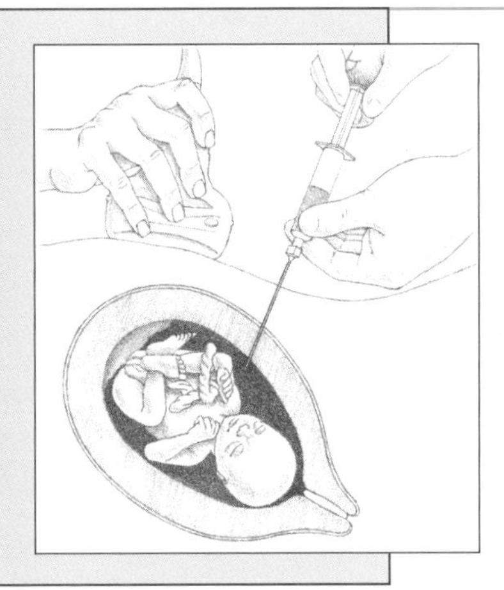

emotions

You will feel much calmer and more in control now the first three months are over and your pregnancy hormones have settled down. Women are often surprised at how energetic and full of life they feel during these middle months of pregnancy.

By weeks 16–18 you will feel your baby move for the first time. Your pregnancy may now begin to feel real, and so it can be a very exciting and emotional experience. It is a good idea to share this milestone moment with your partner.

exercise

Maintain a steady exercise programme. Swimming is a good option as it improves aerobic fitness and muscle tone, but the water supports your weight and encourages slower, more fluid movement, which reduces the likelihood of damaging muscles and joints.

If you normally indulge in potentially dangerous sports such as skiing or horseriding, be aware of the possibility that an accident could have serious and even fatal consequences for your baby. It is therefore best to give these activities a break during your pregnancy.

clothing

During the second trimester you will gain around 6kg (13lb) in weight. This is the time to go shopping for larger, looser garments that will suit your workplace but will also be comfortable enough for you to wear throughout a long day at your work.

You will begin to notice that when you are pregnant you carry your own central heating system, so you may not need to dress as warmly as you used to. In hot weather it is therefore much better to wear cotton fabrics rather than clingy synthetic materials.

serum screening test

Also known as the triple test, this is one of the tests available for giving the 'odds' for the risk of carrying a baby with chromosomal anomaly – most commonly Down's syndrome (see opposite). This blood test is best done between 15–17 weeks and there are now numerous variations on it (double test, triple test, triple plus test etc). The variations are in the number and nature of the chemicals tested for. In general the more chemicals that are tested for, the more cases of abnormality will be found, but there isn't much difference between the tests. Some abnormalities (eg spina bifida, in which the vertebrae of the spine do not close up so the spinal cord is left partially or completely exposed) may be picked up by serum screening, but these abnormalities are not common.

amniocentesis

Usually performed at 16 weeks, this diagnostic test is most commonly used to detect chromosome anomalies, such as Down's syndrome, but many other conditions can also be tested for, such as anencephaly (this is when the majority of the baby's brain and the rear of the skull do not develop). The test is usually done on the basis of your age or if any other tests (nuchal translucency,

Swimming is a wonderful way to both exercise and relax during your pregnancy, as the water supports your weight.

serum screening etc) have indicated a potential problem. Occasionally there is a family history of problems, which makes the test advisable, such as cystic fibrosis or haemophilia. (Cystic fibrosis is a recessive gene disorder of the lungs and the digestive system. Haemophilia is a recessive, gender-linked gene disorder that results in the blood clotting mechanism, factor V111, being absent. Excessive bleeding, internally and externally, results.)

During the procedure the doctor passes a very thin needle through your abdominal wall, after an ultrasound scan has shown where the baby is and whether the placenta is in the path of the needle. About 15ml of amniotic fluid is removed and sent to grow in cell culture in laboratory conditions. This is so the dividing cells can be analysed, and it takes two or three weeks to get a good growth, hence the delay in getting results from the test. There is a 1 per cent (or slightly less) risk of miscarriage as a result of the test. Sadly your baby will be nearly 19 weeks by the time the result is back, and deciding to terminate a pregnancy this late can be very difficult. However, the miscarriage rate for this test, if done any earlier, rises to 3 to 7 per cent and there is also less amniotic fluid available with which to grow a cell culture, so it may have to be done again.

Your partner or chosen companion can usually be present for this test. Women are advised to rest and take it easy for the rest of the day after having it done. You shouldn't experience any ill effects, although some women do have mild abdominal cramping for a few hours afterwards. Very rarely, the cramping is severe, or there is a leak of amniotic fluid from your vagina. If you experience this, you should contact your doctor immediately.

DOWN'S SYNDROME

This condition is mostly caused when an extra chromosome occurs in the body's cells. Each cell normally has 23 pairs of chromosomes (46 in total), apart from the egg cell and the sperm cell, which have 23 in total. In most cases of Down's syndrome there is an extra chromosome in one of the 23 pairs – number 21 – and this alters the genetic information controlling growth and function. Distinctive facial characteristics and varying degrees of mental and physical impairment result. As yet there is no way of reversing the abnormality. One baby in every 800 will be born with this disorder, and the risk rises with increasing maternal age. Tests (see page 30) can discover if a foetus has this condition.

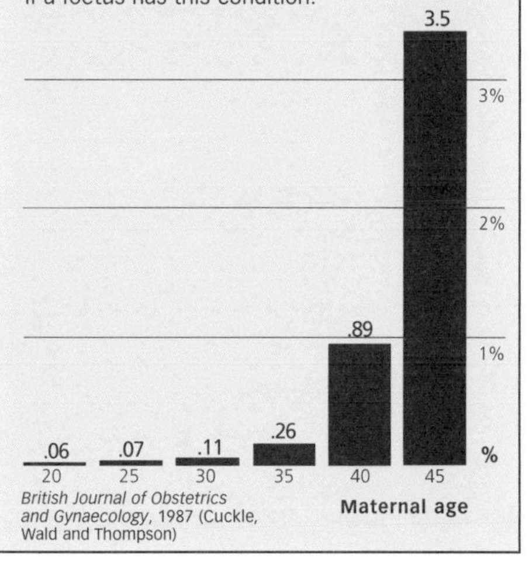

British Journal of Obstetrics and Gynaecology, 1987 (Cuckle, Wald and Thompson)

weeks 17–21

By week 20 you will be halfway through your pregnancy. You may have decided when you intend to take maternity leave, but you should also think about your birth plan and if or when you intend to return to work. Although you don't know how you will feel after your baby is born, there are specific things you can take into account, such as your desire to breastfeed, how demanding your job is and whether there are part-time options available. Discuss this with your partner before approaching your employer.

weeks	lifestyle changes	medical care	diet
17–21	It might seem early to be thinking about cots and changing mats, but it is a good idea to spend some time at this stage checking out what is available and how much it will cost. You won't want to spend your last weeks scouring the shops for baby equipment, as you will be too tired. Don't be persuaded by over-enthusiastic shop assistants to buy too many items at this stage. Ask around at work to see what other women found essential and what they never used, and see if any of your friends and colleagues have second-hand items they can lend to you.	You will probably be offered an ultrasound 'anomaly' scan at this point to check the development of the baby and establish your EDD. The scan only takes approximately 15 minutes, but plan a whole morning or afternoon off work to allow for travel and waiting times. You should also visit your dentist as pregnancy tends to make your gums softer and spongy, so they become vulnerable to infection. National Health dentists provide free treatment during pregnancy and for the first year of your baby's life.	Some women are concerned that pregnancy will change them from being slim to fat after the birth. There is no foundation to this, and, while you will put on weight during the pregnancy, if you are eating a healthy diet then your shape *will* gradually return to normal afterwards. Vegetarians are quite capable of sustaining a healthy pregnancy if they include eggs, around four a week, dairy products and soya in their diet. If you are vegan, take vitamin B12, calcium and vitamin D supplements in tablet form.

your baby

By week 21 your baby will measure about 18cm (7¼in), and will weigh around 300g (nearly 11oz). She is also beginning to fill out a bit now with the formation of fat deposits and her glands are producing a waxy substance called vernix caseosa, which coats the skin to protect her from the amniotic fluid. Your baby also reacts now to touch and pressure that is placed on your abdomen. Although her lungs and digestive system are functioning, they are still very immature.

The baby's taste buds are developing and can tell sweet from bitter.

An ultrasound scan may be able to show the baby's sex at this stage.

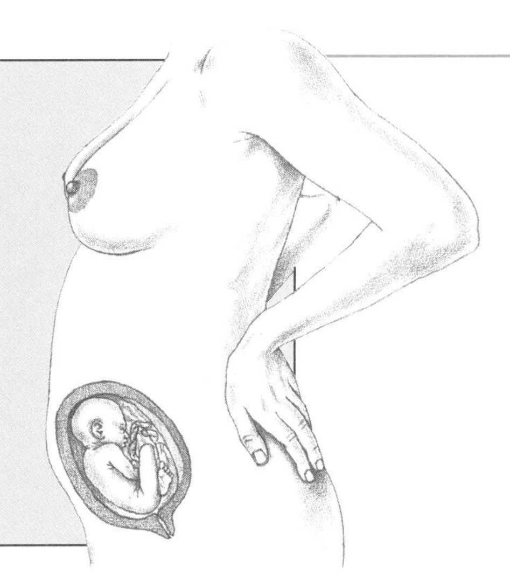

weeks 17–21

emotions

Pregnant women often complain that their brain seems to have stopped functioning. They find concentration hard and forget things easily. This can be upsetting if you are working, because you feel you are less efficient. Don't panic, this is not a permanent absence of brain cells, but is due to the hormones that are now circulating in your body.

To help you through this time, avoid taking on extra commitments, write everything down and take proper time to do tasks. It will take a few weeks after the birth of your baby for you to feel you are back to normal.

exercise

The pelvic floor supports your womb, bladder and bowel so the muscles located here will be under a lot of strain as your baby gets heavier. It is vital to strengthen them in order to avoid stress incontinence (small amounts of urine leak when you cough or sneeze in the later months).

To strengthen your pelvic floor, stop the flow of urine next time you go to the bathroom. The muscles you contract are the muscles you need to exercise. You can exercise them anytime – just contract the muscles and hold this position for as long as possible.

clothing

Shoes are an important consideration when you are pregnant. You will be less stable than usual, and high heels will risk putting your back out as your balance of weight changes. Choose a low-heeled or flat slip-on shoe, which you can remove under your desk.

Your feet and ankles will swell during later months, so don't buy anything too tight-fitting, especially if you are pregnant during hot weather. It is also a good idea to wear trainers on the journey to and from work as they will be much more comfortable and will give you more support for walking.

clothing requirements

You may be wondering how to dress for work now that you are pregnant. You do not need to spend a lot on your pregnancy wardrobe, but a few well-chosen work garments are certainly advisable.

Many office workers these days wear the ubiquitous black trousers or black suit to work and there is no reason why you shouldn't adapt this look. Invest in a couple of pairs of stretchy trousers, or some dark maternity trousers with an expandable waistband. A long-line jacket or knitted jacket is also a useful item, as your thighs and buttocks will be filling out. Opt for loose shirts in natural fabrics that you can dress up to look smart with a scarf and jewellery if necessary. Avoid clingy, synthetic fabrics that will be sweaty and restrictive.

birth plan

The vast majority of births take place in hospital these days, (see page 60), but wherever you deliver you will have choices about how your labour is managed. There are many options that you should think about at this stage. For example, do you want a birthing pool? Do you want to have your baby monitored during labour, which will result in your movement being somewhat restricted? Who do you want with you and are they willing to be there for you? Do you want pain relief and, if so, to what extent? Do you feel strongly about avoiding an episiotomy (the surgical cutting of the opening to the birth canal)? Do you want a natural birth (see page 64)? Ask your doctor or midwife for advice and check that the hospital you have chosen for the birth has the facilities available. If you want to have a home birth, you will need to consult your doctor and midwife early on to find out if they offer this service.

You should also be thinking about finding some domestic support, particularly for the first few weeks after your baby is born. You will need someone to take over a lot of the domestic chores – this person might be your partner, a relative or even paid help (see pages 122–23). Ask the advice of your partner before committing to any arrangement.

ultrasound scan

This painless scan works on the principle of bouncing very high-frequency sound waves off solid objects. The ultrasound scan is used in pregnancy for a number of reasons. It can monitor the growth and development of the baby, establish the expected date of delivery, (if performed before 22 weeks), and detect certain abnormalities of the spine (such as spina bifida), of the skeleton and other organs. It can also establish how your baby and her placenta are lying in the uterus – this information will be important for a trouble-free birth. This could also be when you find out you are having a multiple pregnancy.

Most maternity services offer the first scan between 18–22 weeks, then sometimes again in the middle and at the end of your pregnancy (some maternity services offer earlier scans, eg at 11 weeks or so for the purpose of dating). In certain situations they may be suggested more frequently. Get your partner to attend your first ultrasound scan, because the initial sighting of your baby is a great moment for you both to share.

For the scan you will be asked to lie on your back while your stomach is covered with gel or oil. The operator will then pass an instrument called a transducer across your stomach, picking up high-frequency sound waves, which are then relayed onto a screen to appear as an image of your baby. As far as current research shows, ultrasound will not harm your baby. However it still seems sensible to limit the use of scans.

By this point you may have had a special ultrasound scan that is offered from the 11th week, called a nuchal translucency scan. This is done as an earlier indication of risk than a blood test (see page 30).

The first time you see your baby on the ultrasound scan is a magic moment and one that is best shared with your baby's father if at all possible.

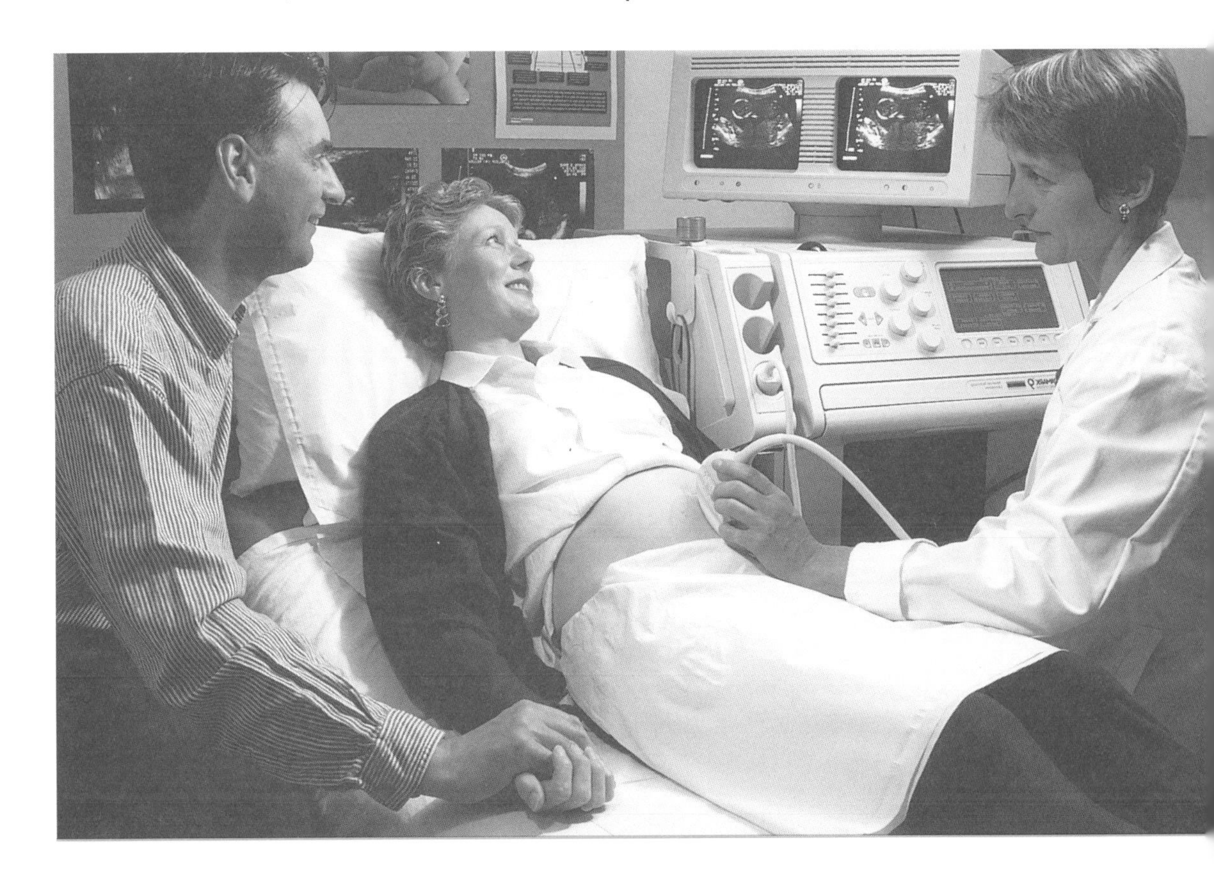

weeks 22–27

By week 27 you are at the six-month mark of your pregnancy, and are also at the beginning of your third trimester. Some women begin to feel quite large at this point, and it can seem a long way to go until your baby is born. Work, unless you are working with other pregnant women, can also seem quite isolating but you should now be looking forward to starting your antenatal classes, which will put you in touch with others who are at the same stage of pregnancy as yourself.

weeks 22–27

lifestyle changes

If driving is part of your job, or you drive to and from work, you can still do this. However, it might become uncomfortable to sit scrunched up in a car for long periods, and you might find your ankles and feet swell. You might also need to urinate more frequently, so factor plenty of stops into any journey you make. Get out and stretch, walk around to get your circulation going and drink bottled water.

Flying is still permissible for another month or two, but avoid light aircraft, which have unpressurized cabins.

medical care

Constipation is frequently a problem throughout pregnancy and particularly in the later stages. This is because the muscles in the bowel are affected by the increased progesterone in pregnancy. Progesterone acts as a relaxant, so your bowel movements slow down and the stools get drier and harder the longer they remain in the bowel. This can be quite difficult if you are at work all day (see page 44).

You will have had your second antenatal appointment by now.

diet

If you are eating a mainly takeaway or canteen diet at work, or have to eat in restaurants as part of your job, you should be aware that much of this prepared food is very high in salt. This also includes supermarket meals such as baked beans and tinned soup. The sodium in salt, if you eat too much, will cause you to retain fluid, which will make your body swell, particularly your hands, feet and ankles.

Choose food without added seasoning and spices to avoid this problem. If in doubt, go for the most straightforward, plain item on the menu.

your baby

By week 27 your baby measures around 24cm (9½in) and weighs 1kg (2lb 3oz). His body is now more in proportion to his head. He will begin to distinguish between light and dark, and be able to open and close his eyes, so he is beginning to practise focusing. His breathing rhythm is now mature, and his lungs are preparing for the first breath outside the womb by developing a lining of special cells. He has probably had the occasional hiccup for some time when he swallows amniotic fluid, but now you might be able to feel it.

He has now developed patterns of sleeping and waking and his skin is no longer translucent.

emotions

Some women become more confident as they get larger, but others find that carrying the extra weight makes them feel self-conscious and unattractive. This feeling can be exacerbated in the work environment if you are surrounded by your sylph-like colleagues in their neat suits and skirts, all talking about their busy social lives.

You might also be worried that you will never get your figure back after the birth. These feelings are normal, but try not to let your shape depress you. It is only temporary, and most women have no problem getting back to normal afterwards.

exercise

Sitting at a desk all day, if you don't take proper breaks, might mean that your ankles and feet will swell and you get cramp in your calf muscles. This is because your circulation is not having a chance to flow properly.

You must get up and move around at least once an hour. When you are sitting down, talking on the phone or working at your computer, raise your feet a little off the floor, flex your feet, and draw circles in the air, first to the right and then to the left. This will help you avoid getting cramp.

clothing

Some women like to wear a maternity girdle during the last three months of pregnancy. If you spend much of your day standing it is worth trying one out, because it will help support the weight of your baby and reduce backache.

Backache commonly occurs because your centre of gravity has altered, which puts a strain on the ligaments of the lower back and pelvis. Make sure the girdle is not too tight around the tops of your thighs, as this can interfere with your circulation. (See page 54 for some further helpful ideas of how to combat backache.)

combating constipation

Constipation is particularly difficult when you are at work all day, because you have less opportunity to empty your bowels when you want to without rushing or feeling self-conscious in the work bathroom facilities.

The best way to avoid constipation is to eat a high-fibre diet, with plenty of fruit and vegetables, and to drink lots of water every day. Keep a large bottle of water by your desk so that you have a regular, fresh supply. If you find that you do have to take laxatives, consult your doctor or pharmacist before using them, because some forms can be inadvisable during pregnancy.

indigestion and heartburn

Pregnant women can suffer from both of these conditions, particularly because the muscle at the entrance to the stomach relaxes with the increased progesterone in the body, just as the other muscles do. When this happens a reflux of stomach acid goes into the oesophagus, which creates the burning sensation of heartburn. And the speed at which food passes through is slowed down, which can prolong the feelings of indigestion. It is best to do what you can to avoid both conditions, as they can cause you to feel very uncomfortable.

To start with, avoid rich, high-fat foods. If you are in a restaurant, then ask for your meat or fish to be plain grilled rather than cooked in a rich, fatty sauce, or choose a large salad or a plate of vegetables dressed with lemon and olive oil. And try eating fruit salad instead of a creamy pudding. This may not seem to be much fun, but then neither is indigestion. Eating a high-fat meal will simply compound the problem and prolong that full feeling, so you should also try to avoid eating a big meal late at night.

Spicy food such as Indian, Thai and Chinese are inadvisable if you are suffering from indigestion and heartburn. The hotness of the food will not be harmful for your baby, but it is sometimes less easy to digest if you are not used to it.

preparing yourself for labour

Around this time, many women begin to focus more on labour and the reality of becoming a mother. Although you have been pregnant for six months, pregnancy can still seem a far cry from parenthood. You can be lulled into a strange feeling that being pregnant is a result in itself, and then one day you wake up with the realization that this bump is going to be born soon, and there is no way back. Not only will you have to go through the drama of labour but the bump will be a separate living, breathing human being and you will be the one responsible for its well-being. The birth of your already very much loved baby will seem incredibly exciting, but also extremely scary.

Will you be able to cope with labour?, you ask yourself. Other women who have already been through it, or who have friends who have, unfortunately often delight in telling grisly stories, but seldom tell you about the normal, straightforward births, where the woman went into hospital at the appointed time, was in labour for a few hours with the requested pain relief and gave birth with no problems to a beautiful and healthy baby. That would be too boring, because happily it is what happens to most of us.

Labour is not a competition, you don't either succeed or fail, it is merely a means to an end. And for most women, labour, even if it has its ups and downs, is overshadowed at the first sight of their beautiful new baby. Don't worry about how you will cope, there is lots of help available when you need it from the medical team and your birth partner. If you made plans for a particular type of birth and it doesn't work out quite that way, for whatever reasons, don't let it upset you. All that matters is that you and your baby are safe and well at the other end.

One of the most important things to remember when having a baby is that you are not alone. Even after the birth, there are many people out there, even if you are without a partner or close family nearby, who are only too willing to help you and your baby with practical and emotional support. So don't be afraid to ask for help if you need it.

who looks after you in labour? If you haven't had much contact with hospitals in the past, they can seem to be rather daunting places, and you might wonder who all the different people in uniforms and white coats are. You may have seen your obstetrician a couple of times during your pregnancy, and he or she heads the team of doctors, nurses and midwives that are in charge of your antenatal care. However, it is unlikely that your obstetrician will attend your baby's birth, as you are more likely to get a more junior doctor, either a registrar or a senior house officer, looking after you.

Occasionally a woman may be asked if it is all right for medical students to attend their antenatal appointments, but you can refuse if you are at all uncomfortable with the idea. Your main carer, however, will be a qualified midwife, who has been thoroughly trained in all aspects of antenatal care, labour and postnatal care.

alternative pain relief You may have been told about visualization exercises in your antenatal classes. These can be extremely effective during labour and it is a good idea to begin practising using them now, so that you are comfortable and natural with them in plenty of time for the birth. Begin by practising associating an active, powerful image with labour. Imagine yourself swimming in the waves, or climbing a mountain peak, and see your physical achievement as exhilarating and empowering. When we focus on the negativity of pain, our bodies close down and become tense, which only increases the level of pain. If you can see labour as a powerful and positive release of your body, an opening out, not a closing down, you will feel less pain. Find some music that reflects these powerful thoughts, and play it often to give you mental strength. And make sure that you take it with you to the delivery room when the time comes.

sex during pregnancy

There is no reason why a couple should not enjoy sex throughout pregnancy, even up until the last minute before labour. However, you may have to experiment with different positions as your 'bump' grows. You should both also be open to the idea of trying new ways of expressing your love, for those times when you don't feel like having full penetrative sex.

Many women do actually find that their sexual appetites increase because of the much higher levels of female hormones, progesterone and oestrogen, coursing through their body, making their breasts and sexual organs more sensitive and responsive. It can even enhance their ability to achieve orgasm, as well as making these occur more frequently. It is also true that many women come to know their body well for the first time during pregnancy, as they face the intimate questions and examinations that go hand in hand with antenatal care. As a result, they begin to truly understand how their body functions. This knowledge can often result in loss of inhibitions and greater sexual freedom.

There are other women, however, who react quite differently, and go off sex completely during pregnancy. Both reactions, and the many in between, are perfectly normal. Some women find they hate their bodies as they begin to change shape and get larger as they no longer feel sexually attractive. Some men feel displaced in their partner's affection by the presence of the 'bump', and this changes their sexual enjoyment. Many couples are scared to make love because they feel it might harm the baby, although this is not the case at all. Whichever way you react, you should realize that your pregnancy is a time of change, not just physically and emotionally for you, but for your partner too, and any change in the individual will bring change to the partnership. You will both feel different about each other once you realize that you share the genes of a new life, and this change can affect the way you approach each other sexually as well as in other aspects of your life.

We are always being fed the idea of perfect sex in advertising and the media, but perfection is a rare thing, and pregnancy may not be the best time to try and achieve it. You are pregnant for such a short proportion of your life, so if there are problems, be patient. What is important is that you can discuss your feelings together, and respect any change in the other's sexual desires. If you do not want sex, then be brave and say so, and settle for physical closeness instead. Cuddle and stroke each other – find comfort in sensuality if not sexuality. There are many ways to make love without having full penetrative sex.

when to avoid sex

Restricting sex during pregnancy should be on the advice of your doctor, but there are some situations when it is sensible, such as if you are experiencing bleeding, if you have a history of miscarriage in the first three months or if you have been diagnosed with placenta praevia (when the placenta attaches to the lower section of the uterus instead of the upper part). If your waters have broken you should not have sex in case you pass an infection to the baby. It is also advisable to restrict sex in the last three months if you are carrying a multiple pregnancy, or have a history of going into labour prematurely.

your baby is safe

Whatever your libido, you will probably find that you want alternative sexual positions as your baby grows. The missionary position – man on top – quickly becomes uncomfortable for the woman. Whatever you choose to try, make sure you are relaxed and unrestricted.

You might worry that sexual intercourse could harm your baby but it is perfectly safe. Your baby is protected by the amniotic sac, in which the fluid cushions him from outside force. This sac is very strong, and would only rupture in extreme circumstances. Your cervix is also closed off with a plug of mucus to prevent the possibility of any infection entering the womb or the amniotic sac. Only after your membranes have ruptured and the plug has been displaced could this be a possibility, but by that time you are in the early stages of labour. Also, the contractions of an orgasm are perfectly safe for a normal pregnancy, and can even be helpful in the later stages because it encourages the uterus to contract. (Orgasm is not thought to bring on labour, unless you are at the point of starting anyway.)

Whatever you decide about sex, be aware of your own needs and don't be pressured by others' attitudes. Make sure you share your feelings with your partner at all times.

Whether you prefer sex or cuddles during your pregnancy, it is important to stay physically close to your partner as your baby develops.

weeks 28–30

You are now at the point in your pregnancy where you could begin your maternity leave if you choose to. Most women work for longer, but there could be any number of reasons why this is a good time for you to stop. If you decide to continue working, you will need to take more care of yourself. The discomforts of pregnancy such as backache, tiredness and indigestion will become more intrusive and you will perhaps be finding the travelling to and from work increasingly tiring.

weeks	lifestyle changes	medical care	diet
28–30	You will need a lot of help and consideration from your family and work colleagues now. If you are a very independent person it may be frustrating, but you should accept all the help you can get. For example, if someone offers you their seat on the train then take it. You will also need to ask someone to lift heavy objects. Avoid carrying piles of work home with you. Shopping should be carried by someone else, even if you still want to choose the items, and any housework that you do should be kept to an absolute minimum. You need to be resting more now.	You will probably be increasing your antenatal appointments from now on to once every fortnight. Cystitis, an infection in the urinary tract, can be more common in pregnancy due to pressure on the bladder and the tubes carrying urine, called ureters. Symptoms include a burning feeling when you urinate or the feeling that you need to urinate, but nothing comes out. There are things you can do to help avoid this – drink plenty of fluids, especially cranberry juice, and urinate as soon as you need to.	You might begin to get hungry late at night now, but eating a big meal late is not a good idea because it will give you terrible indigestion and a sleepless night. However, if you eat a light supper when you get back from work, a snack before bed can relax you and help you sleep. Have a banana sandwich, a biscuit and glass of warm milk, some toast and marmite or a bowl of cereal. If you still find you have a problem, prop yourself up to sleep and eat small, low-fat meals (see page 44 for further ideas of combating indigestion).

your baby

By week 30 your baby will measure almost 26.5cm (10½in) and will also weigh about 1.4kg (3lb). This is still not quite half of her full-term birth weight, but your baby will be putting on weight very fast now. Her brain surface, which up till now has looked smooth, is beginning to develop the grooves an adult brain displays, thus increasing the overall amount of brain surface area. She may also have eyebrows and eyelashes and a head of hair at this stage, although this varies a lot from baby to baby.

Each day she passes as much as ½ litre (I pint) of urine into the amniotic fluid.

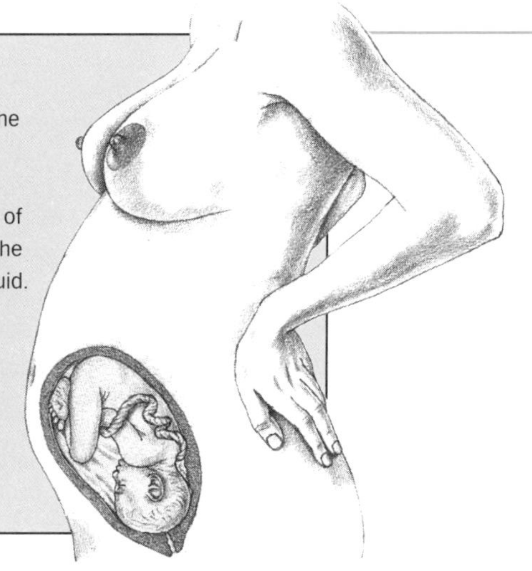

emotions

Your mood swings, after the quiet middle three months, might be back. The pregnancy hormones are still to blame, but add to this tiredness and turmoil about the approaching birth and it is not surprising, particularly if you have a demanding job, that you can get short-tempered and tearful.

If you sense you are getting tense and upset then take a quick break to calm down. Not eating regularly can make you irritable so keep up regular light snacks. And let your partner know how you feel so he can understand why your mood swings.

exercise

Exercising is as much to do with knowing your body and learning how to relax as it is to do with toning and strengthening. This is particularly true with regard to sleep. You may be having difficulty sleeping now, as there no longer seems a comfortable position to lie in.

Taking sleeping pills, even herbal ones, is not an option for you except in extreme circumstances, and then not without consulting your doctor first, because of the possible effect on your baby. However, it does help to find a comfortable position in which to lie (see page 51).

clothing

Vaginal secretions increase during pregnancy, and most women experience some vaginal discharge at times. This is normal if it does not contain blood, or cause itching, redness, soreness or a strong smell. If you experience any of these you should see your doctor.

Because of the normal, increased vaginal discharge it is advisable to wear a pantyliner when going to work, and to keep a supply of them at the office. Using any sort of tampons or vaginal deodorants is not appropriate because of the risk of infection or irritation.

learning to relax

Relaxation is vital at this stage in pregnancy. It will not only help in labour, but it is also a way to unwind those tired muscles at the end of a long working day. So when you get home, take half an hour to relax. Lie on your side with your back and your tummy well-supported, legs and arms comfortably bent. Alternatively, sit in a comfortable chair. Close your eyes and concentrate on different areas of your body, starting with your feet. Very gently tense your muscles, then relax them. Work your way up your body doing the same to each muscle group, paying most attention to areas where you carry tension, such as your neck, shoulders and back.

You should also get a partner or a friend to give you a massage, as massaging any part of your body soothes away tensions and improves circulation. And, by the sixth month, your baby will be able to sense the stroking touch through your abdomen and will also be

Your body is under increasing strain as your baby grows, so find ways to soothe away aches and pains when you get home.

soothed by it. Choose an essential oil used in aromatherapy, and dilute it with a light vegetable oil to 1.5 per cent. Lavender or rose are both good after the sixth month, but there are many essential oils that are not advised as they can induce menstrual flow or be potentially toxic for your baby. Always check with a qualified aromatherapist or herbalist before using oils.

You could try an unscented oil such as almond oil, which doesn't have the benefits of essential oils but is safe to use.

sleeping arrangements

Learn to sleep on your side – lying on your back or your stomach is no longer a good idea as the baby's weight will make this uncomfortable. Make sure your room is well ventilated and your bedclothes are not too heavy, otherwise you will get too hot. If you are worried about disturbing your partner if you are particularly restless, suggest he sleeps in the spare room.

your skin

Stretch marks, called striae, can appear on the tummy, breasts, buttocks and thighs. They can look alarmingly dark brown or purple during pregnancy, but this colour fades afterwards to a pale silver, although the marks will probably never completely disappear. There is no way of predicting who will get stretch marks and who won't, although age, skin condition, general health, size and the amount of weight you put on during pregnancy are all possible factors. Rub an easily absorbed cream (without active ingredients) or ordinary vegetable oil into your stomach every day to keep your skin supple. Although this is no guarantee your skin will not mark, it will keep it in the best condition for the stretching it has to do.

Itchy skin is very common, particularly on the stomach as the skin stretches. You will feel it more intensely if the weather is hot or you are wearing synthetic fabrics that don't allow your skin to breathe. Use calamine lotion or rub your skin with a light cream or oil after washing, and avoid strongly scented soap or bath oil. If the itching is very bad and starts to spread, then consult your doctor. There is a condition called obstetric cholestasis, a liver malfunction, which presents with intense itching and can have serious consequences if not treated.

Your skin can show various changes during pregnancy. Most pregnant women have a beautiful fullness and bloom brought about by the change in hormones, which makes the skin softer and smoother, and often reduces spots. However, you may get tiny spider veins on your face and body or darker facial areas of skin, known as chloasma. Both will fade postnatally. Rashes, particularly beneath your breasts as they get heavier, or between your thighs where extra weight can cause chafing, can be a problem, especially if you are cooped up behind a desk all day and aren't moving around. Try to keep your skin clean and dry and nip any problems in the bud with calamine lotion or unscented talcum powder.

weeks 31–33

Even if you are working up until the last moment, you will be beginning to think about handing over to whoever will be doing your job when you are on maternity leave. Your main focus is probably your baby now, and his size will be a constant reminder, but some women do worry about leaving work. You may be feeling that the person taking over from you will do the job too well and that they won't want you back. But you must pack up and go with confidence, as this is one of the biggest adventures of your life!

weeks	lifestyle changes	medical care	diet
31–33	Air travel is perhaps not a good idea now, although some airlines will take pregnant women up until the 36th week with a doctor's letter confirming there are no apparent complications. You will probably find that sitting belted up in a cramped space with dry, recycled air, no room to move about, and the possibility of turbulence very unpleasant. Also, if you are abroad and you go into labour, you will be far from the support network you have built up over the previous months. It is best to travel within a 45-minute radius of home and hospital.	You should be starting weekly antenatal classes by week 31, if you haven't already done so. Encourage your partner to go with you as it will benefit him too (see page 17). Your breasts will not only have grown bigger, but the nipples will probably have darkened and have a more waxy texture from the oily secretions from the glands in the nipples. They may also be leaking tiny amounts of colostrum, your baby's first milk. To prepare your breasts for breastfeeding, avoid washing them with soap, dry them well and rub them with a rich cream or body lotion.	The strong desire to eat things that are not actually foodstuffs is known as pica, and can come on in the later stages of pregnancy. For instance, women have been known to crave soil or coal. This is said to be the body responding to a lack of vitamins or minerals, and appears to be less common now that women eat more nutritious diets. It is also not unusual for women to crave normal foodstuffs, such as ice cream or pickled gherkins, and it is fine to indulge in these cravings in moderation. Just make sure that you don't overdo things.

your baby

By week 33 your baby measures nearly 31cm (12in). He weighs around 2kg (4lb 6oz) and has probably turned and settled in the head-down position (vertex), which he will stay in until his birth (an ultrasound scan will pick up if he hasn't – don't be alarmed if this happens; some babies turn very late). His face is now smoother and less wrinkled. If he were to be born now he would have a very high probability of survival in an incubator, although his lungs are still immature and he cannot maintain his body temperature unaided.

The baby is supplied with oxygen via the placenta and circulates his blood back to his mother.

Key
oxygenated blood
deoxygenated blood
mixed blood

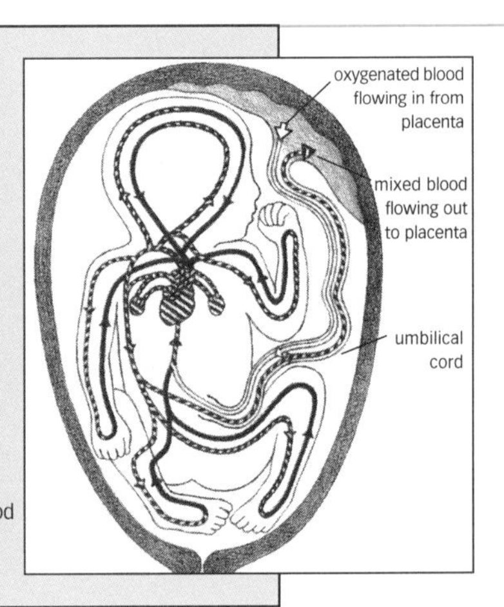

emotions

Changing to the home environment from work might feel strange at first. You will be busy getting the baby's room ready with new equipment, but then time may hang heavy as you wait for labour to begin. You will probably miss your colleagues and feel slightly odd without your normal routine. You may find you rely more heavily on your partner's company.

If you have met women you like at antenatal classes in your area, suggest meeting up to compare notes. If you have a friend or relative who has a small baby, spend time with them.

exercise

If you haven't been following an exercise regime during pregnancy, then don't start now. Stick to a daily routine of gentle walks. You may also find that you have to moderate any workout you have been doing. This is because your muscles will be under increasing strain from your rapidly growing baby.

Stress incontinence can be a problem for some women at this time so make sure you start pelvic floor exercises if you haven't already. If you find that you do suffer from occasional incontinence, wear a sanitary pad.

clothing

You are carrying a lot of excess weight now, and might well be suffering from aching legs. If so, it is worth investing in a pair of support tights. These should be put on early in the day, before your legs begin to ache and swell, and will relieve much of the discomfort as well as improve circulation. These tights are particularly helpful if you are prone to varicose veins (see page 54).

weeks
31–33

varicose veins

It is quite common for women in the later stages of pregnancy to have varicose veins to some degree. Your susceptibility will depend a lot on whether you have a history of varicose veins in your family, if you spend too long on your feet, how old you are and how much weight you have put on in ratio to your size. The varices are caused by blood getting trapped in the veins in the legs because of reduced blood flow away from the legs. This happens due to the pressure from the baby. The veins then get engorged and the vein walls become weak and bulgy.

If you are having problems with varicose veins, then wear support tights and avoid standing up for too long. Sitting still in the same position or with your legs crossed also impedes circulation. While sitting, keep your legs raised, if at all possible, to allow the blood flow to improve.

In general, beware of any restrictive clothing that might hinder blood flow and therefore increase the likelihood of swelling, such as rings, tight sleeves and socks or pants with tight bands. If your hands, feet or face suddenly become very swollen and puffy, consult your doctor, as it could be a sign of pre-eclamptic toxaemia (see page 31 for a description of this).

backache

Most women experience some back pain during their pregnancy. This is because the burden of extra weight from your baby presses on the discs in the lower spine and reduces the fluid that cushions them, especially if you are standing or sitting a lot. To avoid this happening, you should move around frequently during the day and take the weight off your spine at regular intervals by lying on your side or getting on all fours with your back flat, not hollowed. If you do have to sit for long periods, make sure that your back is well supported with a small cushion.

Poor posture is also a common cause of back pain. Round shoulders, weak stomach muscles and a tense neck and jaw all contribute to backache (as the muscles are all interrelated), which is then exacerbated by the imbalance and extra weight you are carrying in your stomach and breasts when pregnant. Be extremely vigilant about watching your posture while you are pregnant. With the increasing weight you may find that you tend to poke your stomach forward and arch your back. This will cause dreadful backache and it actually isn't necessary to use such stiff, exaggerated movements just because you are pregnant. Learn to stand tall, as if an invisible thread is attached to the crown of your head, pulling you gently upwards. Your shoulders should be relaxed, stomach muscles strong and your neck and jaw flexible (see the exercises on page 71).

Right: Maintain a good, straight posture, and make sure you don't sit scrunched up – this will protect you from backache.

weeks 34–36

It's getting close now, by week 36 you will only have four weeks to go. Your baby will probably descend around this time, its head engaging in your pelvis ready for labour. This will mean that your bump will drop down from lying right up under your breasts and you might find breathing easier. The down side is that your baby will be pressing on your bladder more, which means frequent trips to the bathroom, and disturbed nights. Get as much rest as possible during the day if you are not sleeping well at night.

weeks	lifestyle changes	medical care	diet
34–36	Now is the time for you to pack your bag ready for the hospital as there is a chance your baby could be born anytime from now on (see page 58 for a detailed list of what should go into your bag). If you are still working, you should make sure that you have organized everything at home and that someone is on hand to pick up your hospital bag if you begin your labour while you are at work. Your colleagues will probably be regarding you with some trepidation by now, just in case you do go into labour while you are with them, rather than at home.	You will be starting weekly antenatal check-ups from week 36. The doctor or midwife will be confirming whether your baby is in the best position for a straightforward labour, that the head is beginning to engage and that she is lying curled up with her face towards your back. If her bottom or legs are down (breech) instead of her head, or she is lying across your tummy (transverse lie), the medical staff will want to monitor you very carefully over the next few weeks and might suggest the possibility of a caesarean section (see pages 58 and 59).	Small meals that are eaten often are essential at this stage to avoid indigestion and heartburn and to keep your level of calories up so that you are strong and fit for labour and your first weeks as a new mother. You probably won't feel like cooking, so choose lots of easy-to-prepare fresh salads and vegetables, and meat, fish or chicken that you can stick under the grill with the minimum of fuss. If your partner wants something more elaborate, then suggest he cooks it, as well as preparing yours too.

your baby

By week 36 your baby will measure top to toe around 46cm (18in) and weigh about 2.75kg (6lb). She is putting on weight fast, around 250g (8oz) each week. Although her length is nearly that of a full-term baby, her arms and legs are still much thinner. The vernix caseosa (waxy coating) and lanugo (fine hair), which has been covering the baby to waterproof her skin, has almost disappeared. Her fingernails have grown to reach the end of her fingers and her eyes are now blue.

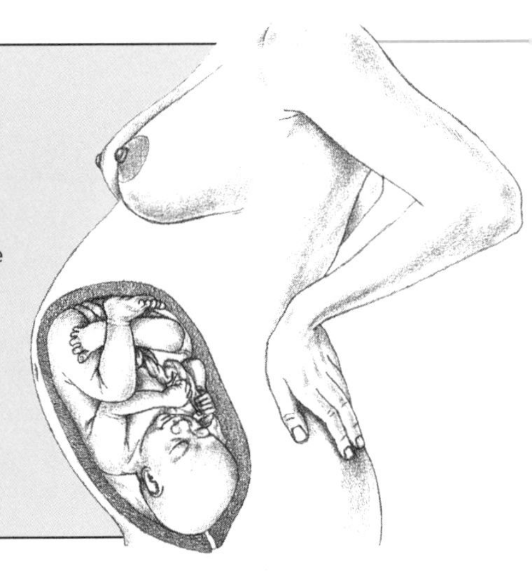

She won't be moving so much now, as there isn't enough space for her limbs to uncurl.

emotions

Your emotions might be up and down, but what about your partner's? A man is often in awe of his heavily pregnant spouse and doesn't know what to do with her. He finds her mood swings incomprehensible, and worries that it's his fault; he is terrified of labour and seeing her in pain; and the prospective responsibility of being a family rather than a couple can be overwhelming.

You may be so absorbed in your own body and its dramas that you don't realize that your partner is in a nervous state too. Make sure you talk to him as you both need each other's support.

exercise

The main thing in these last weeks is to keep moving. If you have just given up work and no longer need to gear yourself up every day, it is easy just to completely relax at home and stop even the most rudimentary effort.

Try to develop some home exercises to keep you supple and strong for labour. Do some gentle stretching and relaxing and try walking or swimming. Whatever you do, don't allow your aerobic strength to weaken or your body to get stiff.

clothing

If you have decided to breastfeed, even if just for the first few weeks, you will need to buy at least two nursing bras. You can wear these in the later stages of pregnancy as well, as they offer support both for day and night. A good nursing bra is front-fastening, with cups that undo to give you easy access. After the baby is born you will also need disposable pads that fit in the cups to soak up any leaking milk.

Some hospitals supply nappies and gowns for your baby, but check beforehand. You will need something to dress her in when you leave.

packing for hospital

Before you prepare your bag with what you will need while you are in hospital, it is a good idea to keep a list that you can add to as you remember things you will need both during and after labour. Always pack well in advance so that you are not caught out if you do go into labour early. To help you with your arrangements, here is a list of the basic things you will probably want: an old T-shirt and loose socks to wear in labour; a flannel or sponge, lip salve, a spray bottle for spraying your face with cool water and magazines and books to read in case you're kept hanging about. You should also have snacks such as wholefood bars and cartons of juice, two nighties with buttons at the front for breastfeeding, two nursing bras with disposable pads, extra pillows, soft toilet paper, lots of pants and heavy-duty sanitary pads, as you will lose some blood, known as lochia, in the first few days. Also pack a dressing gown and slippers and toiletries, including shampoo. You will need coins or cards for the phone and a list of phone numbers of the people you will want to contact as soon as you have had your baby. You must also remember to have a baby seat fitted into your car for when you go home.

medical intervention

As well as normal pain relief during labour (see page 67), there are other medical procedures that might be appropriate.

caesarean section This is an operation where the baby is delivered through a surgical

MEDICAL REASONS FOR A CAESAREAN SECTION

- If the baby is deemed very big, or the mother's pelvis size inadequate, suggesting a mismatch (known as cephalo-pelvic disproportion). This is very difficult to predict accurately before labour, and would usually be a reason for emergency caesarean section.
- If the baby is in an abnormal position, such as breech or transverse lie, and cannot be turned before labour.
- If the baby is in distress, possibly because of protracted labour.
- If the placenta is blocking the birth canal, known as placenta praevia.
- A prolapsed umbilical cord, which is when the cord enters the birth canal before the baby's head. It becomes compressed and therefore threatens the baby's blood supply.
- Previous caesarean section, where there is danger of the uterus rupturing during a normal labour. This reason on its own is now seen by many obstetricians as outdated as you do not necessarily have to have a caesarean second time round. If you have had a caesarean before and want a vaginal birth this time, discuss this with your doctor.

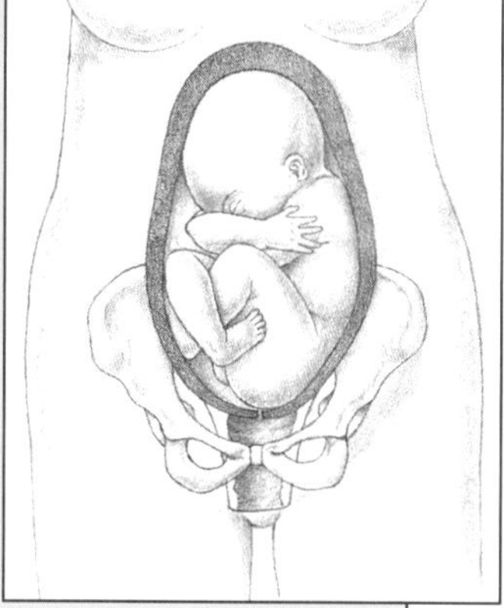

If your baby is in a breech position, you may need a caesarean.

incision in the abdominal wall. It can be done under an epidural anaesthetic, spinal block, or, infrequently, general anaesthetic. It can either be elective, which means that your doctor decided at some time during the pregnancy that it would be wise for you not to go through a vaginal delivery, or it can be an emergency, which means it is carried out as a result of problems either for you or the baby during labour itself.

A caesarean section, although not complicated to perform, is a major operation, and carries all the possible risks of major surgery, such as post-operative infection, pain, blood loss and injury to other organs such as the bladder or rectum. There is also a much longer recovery rate than there is from having a normal vaginal birth with the attendant problems of dealing with a small baby while recovering from surgery.

In the last 30 years the number of caesarean sections performed, both elective and emergency, has risen dramatically in the developed world. This is due to the improved detection of problems through ultrasound scans and good antenatal care, and the fact that women are giving birth to bigger babies than ever before because of better nutrition and less smoking during pregnancy. But there is another factor: some patients (and doctors too) who are both busy and stressed, want to fit the baby's birth round their schedules and like the convenience of planning a caesarean. Many women are also anxious about labour, and equally worried that giving birth vaginally will mean they are less sexually appealing afterwards. These are not necessarily sensible or appropriate reasons for choosing a caesarean section. If your doctor suggests one, make sure there is a valid medical reason before agreeing to it.

epidural anaesthetic During this procedure, local anaesthetic is injected into the epidural space, which lies outside the dura – the membrane round the spinal cord. An area of skin in your lower back over your spinal cord is numbed with local anaesthetic, then a hollow needle is introduced to the epidural space, through which anaesthetic is delivered. A tiny plastic catheter is also placed in the space and left there to allow for any necessary top ups of local anaesthetic. An epidural should reduce sensation from your waist down, and provide pain relief without you losing consciousness.

The disadvantages of this option include the lowering of your blood pressure, which can affect the baby's blood supply, and reducing your urge to push in the second stage, which can result in a forceps delivery. You may also experience headaches and backache afterwards due to the medication and possible bruising in the injection site.

spinal block This is when the needle, instead of being placed in the epidural space, is passed deeper, so that a spinal block can be created. This is the technique that is the most recommended for caesarean section, as it has the ability to produce a rapid and highly effective degree of pain relief.

where to have your baby

Most births, especially for first babies, take place in hospital these days. In Britain more than 95 per cent of all births are hospital deliveries. However, you do have choices about where you have your baby, who will be present and what monitoring system you want to use. If you are particularly inclined to a certain type of birth, then it is best to discuss it with the midwife as soon as possible.

hospital birth

If you decide on a hospital birth, you can still make choices about how you would like your labour and aftercare to proceed, and it is wise to choose your hospital based on those decisions. Although it would be foolish to pick one at some distance from your home, the nearest one might not be the best for you. If you want a natural birth, then you don't want to go to a hospital that frowns on this idea. If you want a water birth, it is best to choose one where this method is a normal procedure. Some hospitals that don't offer this facility will let you take your own pool in.

You should check the policies of the various hospitals in your area regarding induction, pain relief, foetal monitoring and partner participation. Visit the labour units and maternity wards in the local hospitals and opt for the one with the most conducive atmosphere. There are many issues to consider. You might prefer the atmosphere of a smaller, more intimate hospital in your area, rather than a larger complex. You might want a particular doctor or midwife to oversee the birth, and should therefore choose the hospital to which they are attached. If you are in the Domino scheme (see glossary, page 156), you need to check which of your local hospitals this operates in. If you want to breastfeed, you should look for a hospital where you will be supported with advice on technique and potential problems in the first vital days after the birth.

Shaving the perineum, the area around the vagina, routinely before delivery has been largely discontinued in most hospitals, so if it is suggested you can refuse.

home birth

Since the beginning of the 1990s, increasing numbers of women have chosen to deliver at home, although the numbers still remain small. Women who take this step consider the experience to be much more cosy and relaxed, with less medical intervention and more contact with siblings. There is unfortunately still considerable prejudice among health professionals, usually based on very inadequate evidence, against home births. Many doctors feel, for example, that home births are not appropriate for a first labour, while the evidence shows that home birth is an entirely reasonable option for many women having their first baby. Increasingly GPs are not prepared to be involved in home births, but don't let this dissuade you; it will be your midwife who will assist with your labour and delivery in any case. It is certainly advisable for both you and your partner to be happy with the decision, though.

There are without doubt some conditions that would make a home birth inadvisable such as pre-eclampsia, pregnancy diabetes, pre-existing illnesses such as heart or kidney disease, a multiple birth, breech presentation and significant haemorrhage during the pregnancy but your midwife or doctor will be able to advise you further on this.

monitoring during labour

When you check into hospital for labour, you will probably be examined vaginally to see how far your cervix has dilated, be made comfortable in your own labour clothes or in a hospital gown and your baby's heart rate will be checked. Many hospitals will routinely check the heart rate for a while (at least 20 minutes) with an external foetal heart rate monitor (EFM), which is an ultrasound monitor that is strapped to your abdomen and which electronically generates a print-out called a cardiotocograph (CTG). In an uncomplicated labour there is good evidence that there is no need to continue this CTG if it is normal, and the baby's heart rate can be monitored intermittently. This has the clear advantage that you can remain mobile and so are not confined to a bed, and you can also get into a bath if you wish. If there are valid reasons for continuing the CTG it will remain on, and if it is felt that the quality of the recording is inadequate there may be a case for applying a clip electrode to your baby's scalp. With increasingly sophisticated and reliable trans-abdominal monitors the need for these clips to be applied has now been greatly reduced.

The overuse of CTGs has also undoubtedly resulted in unnecessary anxiety in many labours, which means that caesarean sections and other interventions that may not be necessary have occurred. Hand-held ultrasound monitors provide a totally acceptable alternative to the EFM in most normal labours.

birth partner

Your birth partner, whether it is the baby's father or a trusted friend, has a vital part to play in labour, so you need to make sure that they are briefed thoroughly about your birth plan in advance. If possible, try to take them to the delivery room and introduce them to your team of attendants too, as it will help them to feel part of the team.

Whoever your birth partner is, he or she will need to be strong in the face of your pain and the intensity of labour, and must be able to put up with any outbursts from you. They can hold you, fetch things for you and reassure you during what will be an extraordinary and memorable experience for you both.

weeks 37–40

This is it, the final days before you get to see your baby face to face for the first time. You will perhaps be swinging between longing to get it all over, and dreading the actual moment that it will start. Every night you will go to sleep wondering whether tonight's the night, and part of you hopes it will be while the other part just wants one more good sleep. You will probably be getting increasingly impatient as you just have to sit back and wait for it to happen now.

weeks	lifestyle changes	medical care	diet
37–40	A lot of women, when they give up work, concentrate on the baby's room, to make sure they have all the equipment and that it's ready. But you mustn't neglect other things that should be sorted out, not just for your stay in hospital, but for the first weeks after the birth when you will only want to deal with your baby. For example, have you stocked up the freezer with some handy meals for when you come home? Have you written a list of the people you or your partner will want to call when the baby has been born? Has the car got petrol in it?	You will probably be anxious about unusual aches or pains now, wondering if they are the onset of labour. Some women do experience false labour. In the last few weeks you might notice Braxton Hicks contractions (see glossary, page 156), but these are not a sign of imminent labour. Some recognizable signs of labour are longer, more regular, frequent and painful contractions; you have a show: the plug of pinkish mucus from the neck of the cervix; or your waters break. The latter normally occurs later, but it can sometimes be the first sign.	You will hopefully have maintained a good level of nutrition throughout the previous months, and are fit and healthy for the birth. Therefore allow yourself your favourite treats in these last weeks, but don't overdo them. You still need to watch your nutrition as the baby is growing and taking a lot from you. There also won't be a lot of room in your stomach for food at this stage, so make sure that you keep your meals small and regular. Even if you have swollen legs and feet you must keep your fluid intake up, with at least five glasses of water a day.

your baby

By week 40 your baby is ready to be born. Unfortunately the due date is only a guide, and most first babies are later rather than earlier than their EDD. The average newborn will measure between 44–55cm (18–22in) and weigh 2.5–5kg (5½–11lb). He will have bulked out a lot in the last few weeks and be very tightly curled in your womb. He will probably also feel very heavy now. All his organs and systems are capable of functioning outside the womb but the lungs are the last thing to reach maturity.

His intestine now contains a greeny black substance called meconium, which will be his first bowel movement, after (or sometimes before) his birth.

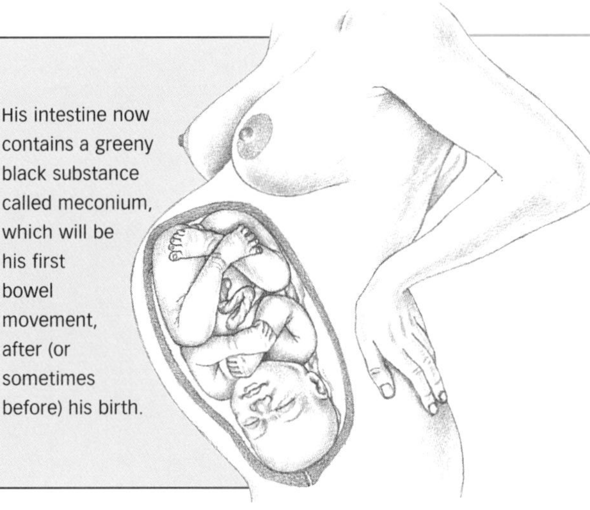

weeks 37–40

emotions

You will probably be in a fragile emotional state by the end of your pregnancy. You will feel enormous and may be short-tempered. It is also hard to handle the uncertainty of when labour might begin. It colours everything, from lunch with a friend to a trip to the shops. If your baby is overdue, this nervous anticipation can become quite wearing.

Don't put yourself under any extra emotional strain. If there is an irritating friend or relative wanting your attention, be firm – this is not the time to tax yourself with someone else's demands.

exercise

Sitting around worrying about labour can make you tense. Practise your breathing for labour, which will not only make you more confident about dealing with the event, but will also help to relax you in the moments when you do start to worry.

Keep yourself moving with gentle exercise such as walking short distances, doing the leg and ankle mobilizer (see page 73) and shoulder rolls (see page 79). Make sure you do not sit cramped up in one place for too long without getting up and moving around.

clothing

You will be heartily sick and tired of your pregnancy clothes by now. Most women have a very limited wardrobe for the last weeks and you can grow to hate that baggy T-shirt, or those bulging pregnancy trousers.

There's no point in buying anything new now, but within a few weeks you will begin to feel physically like yourself again, and, even if your pre-pregnancy clothes do not fit for a while, you will at least be able to buy the odd garment that is not maternity clothing to see you through until you have your old shape back.

birth choices

Whatever choices you have made about how and where to have your baby, these plans may be thwarted at the last minute by birth complications, timing and where you are when you go into labour, so try not to be too rigid in your desires. Every woman would like every detail of her labour to go as planned, but it doesn't usually work that way.

natural childbirth You may decide that you want a natural birth, without the intervention of any sort of artificial procedures such as drugs for pain relief, oxytocin to accelerate labour, a caesarean section or an episiotomy (see below). If you are keen to go down this route then you will have already attended natural childbirth classes and explored the different techniques for pain relief such as relaxation, visualization, massage, hypnosis, acupuncture and homeopathic remedies. However, it might be essential, for the well-being of both you and your baby, that you have medical intervention during labour. This should not be seen as a failure. State your desires to the team caring for you, but if there comes a moment when, for instance, an epidural is preferable, then don't feel guilty. Having a baby is an inexact science, and all that matters in the end is that both you and your baby are healthy.

episiotomy An episiotomy is the surgical cutting, under local anaesthetic, of the opening to the birth canal. This procedure is done to avoid tearing in the area as the baby's head is born. However, it is no longer routinely performed and most women do prefer not to have one, as the site of the episiotomy can continue to cause some level of discomfort for quite some time after the actual birth. In some cases it can also lead to complications if the stitching is too tight or if the stitches have become infected.

A carefully managed second stage, in which your vaginal opening is allowed to stretch gradually in order to accommodate the baby's head, can help prevent tearing, but you will not actually know for sure whether an episiotomy is necessary until the second stage of labour. If your baby's head is very big, or the doctor needs to do a forceps delivery, it is often the best option. You should tell your doctor if you are totally against having an episiotomy, but, even if you are, you should also be prepared to have one if the need arises.

water birth A water birth is no longer considered an 'alternative' method of birthing, although there are still some hospitals that do not offer this facility, and some obstetricians who are not happy with the method. Warm water is actually a very natural way of relaxing and easing contractions during labour. Some hospitals will even allow you to deliver in the water, while others prefer to deliver the baby out of the water and therefore just use the pool for the earlier stages of labour and for pain relief. Check with your doctor or midwife as to the policy of your chosen hospital, but if you really want

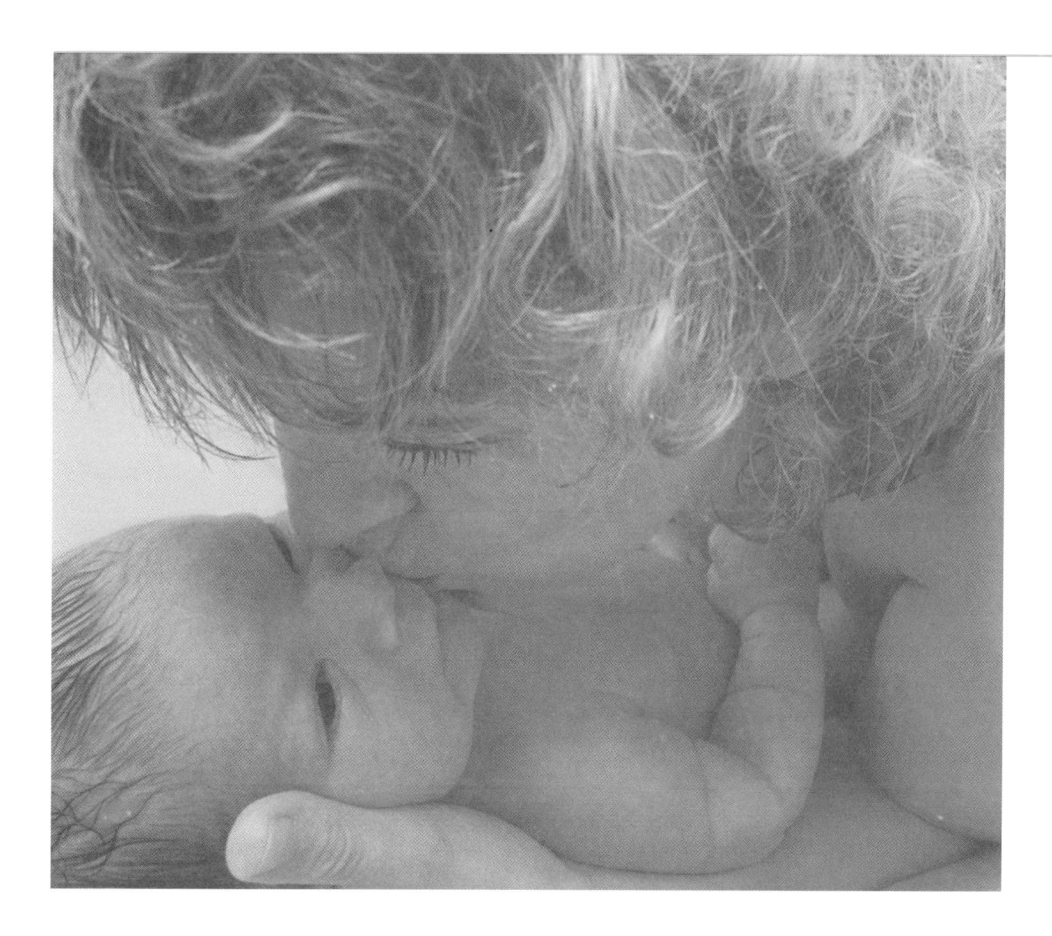

a water birth then you must make sure you choose a hospital that has a well-established track record with the process.

Although it is a very soothing, safe way of giving birth, there are a few disadvantages of having a water birth. These include the slight increase in the chance of postnatal infection for your baby, fears that the baby will inhale water from the pool (although this does not appear to happen in reality) and the fact that the midwife cannot monitor the progress of the baby in the second stage if you are submerged in water, which sometimes results in unnecessary vaginal tearing. You will also not be able to be attached to any continuous foetal monitoring system while you are in the water because of the danger of an electrical charge, which can rule the method out if the team think your baby might be at risk. However, your baby can still be monitored intermittently in the pool if the midwife uses a hand-held monitor.

Holding your newborn baby in your arms for the first time makes all the waiting and wondering finally worthwhile.

what happens during labour

The time is fast approaching when you will be giving birth to your new baby. You will be filled with a mixture of emotions, including excitement but also apprehension about what will happen and what the pain will be like. The level of pain can vary enormously and no one is able to predict how you will react to the intensity of labour. The different stages of labour are explained below to put your mind at rest, and the types of pain relief available are also explored.

the three stages of labour

No one can predict how long your labour will go on for, but with a first pregnancy there is an average, only an average, of 12 hours (it is usually shorter in later pregnancies).

first stage This is when your cervix, which is the fibrous (slightly muscular) ring at the neck of the womb, begins to soften and dilate to allow the baby's passage. The uterus begins to produce prostaglandin at this time to stimulate contractions. As the contractions push the baby's head or presenting part onto the stretching cervix, oxytocin is also produced, which results in regular contractions. It is best to remain in an upright position at this point and to move around, as this will encourage the production of oxytocin and help the contractions to progress. If your first stage is too slow, you might be given extra oxytocin via an intravenous drip to speed up your contractions. By the end of this stage they will be coming strongly, and the cervix will have dilated to 10cm (4in).

second stage There will be a brief transition time between the first and second stage when the cervix is fully dilated and the womb is preparing to push your baby out. This might last for a couple of contractions and go almost unnoticed, or it might be a more protracted period when you feel irritable, flushed and nauseous, and you may also have a powerful urge to open your bowels.

Next follows a much more exciting time when you can begin to push and the end is in sight. Although this stage is relentless, most women find it more bearable than the endless contractions of the first stage. The desire to push is not a choice but an irresistible and overwhelming reflex urge that takes over your whole body and results in the birth of your baby.

third stage You will probably be so excited that your baby has been born that you won't notice your uterus continuing to contract until it shrinks down into a ball near the level of your umbilicus and the placenta peels away from the lining of the womb. This occurs within five minutes of the birth, and it is frequently speeded up by an intramuscular injection of oxytocin, which most hospitals administer routinely immediately after your baby is born. These contractions also help to close down the blood vessels in the uterus after the placenta has separated.

pain relief during labour

Apart from epidural anaesthetic, which has already been discussed (see page 59), there are other forms of drug relief suitable for labour that are commonly available in most hospitals. Be aware that, whatever pain relief you choose, all drugs pass into your baby's bloodstream and affect him to some degree.

entonox 'Gas and air' is a very common form of pain relief during labour. Entonox is a mixture of 50 per cent nitrous oxide (a weak anaesthetic and pain-killing gas) and 50 per cent oxygen and it is inhaled through a rubber mask that you administer yourself. It offers mild pain relief and the effect is felt within 30 seconds of inhalation but usually lasts no more than a minute. Useful at the first sign of a contraction, it helps you over the worst peak. Reactions vary from detachment, mild euphoria, a floating sensation to nausea. This form of pain relief is said not to harm the baby as it is quickly removed from the baby's bloodstream in the first breaths he takes outside the womb.

pethidine Pethidine is a narcotic drug, given either by intravenous or intramuscular injection, and it is both a sedative and an analgesic because it relaxes and distances the pain. You may feel quite woozy and out of control with this drug, or just sleepy. Unfortunately it is not effective for some women. Pethidine can cause nausea and is usually given in combination with another drug to counteract the nausea. (Some hospitals may use alternative drugs that are similar to pethidine.)

Pethidine is not so useful in the second stage of labour, because it reduces your desire to push effectively. The effect of pethidine lasts from two to four hours, and can suppress your baby's respiratory function, which means that some babies need to have help with their breathing after birth if the drug is administered in the five hours before delivery.

tens Trans-cutaneous Electrical Nerve Stimulation is a device that delivers small electrical currents to the nerves to block pain and stimulate endorphins – chemicals that are the body's natural pain killers. Electrodes are placed on the skin, usually on the lower back, and you control the amount of current you receive with a handset.

It is best to start using TENS in early labour, and, although it does not relieve pain as such, it can help you cope with contractions by altering your perception of the pain. Machines are available in most hospitals, but you may have to book one in advance. It does not, however, seem to work for everyone.

Up until now you may not have considered the issue of safety at work particularly seriously unless your job is in an obviously hazardous arena such as construction, or you are dealing with radiation or dangerous chemicals. But now you are pregnant, there are conditions, which would not necessarily have serious implications for a woman who is not pregnant, that might affect the health and safety of your baby. In this section we look at general categories of risks for pregnant women, and also at some specific workplace situations.

Your home environment is one that you can control. You decide whether it is a no-smoking household, whether you take proper precautions when doing building work and how chemicals will be stored. There is no pressure on you to put yourself at risk from lifting heavy objects or dealing with complex machinery. And if you get tired and worn out, you can stop what you are doing and take a short rest.

At work, however, you are at the mercy of your employer and the environment the company has created. This might be a safe and healthy one, where the employers are prepared to listen to the needs of their workforce, but it might not, and many people, particularly women, find it difficult to stand up for themselves in the workplace, and as a result subject themselves to unnecessary hazards, worrying that they will lose their job if they don't.

Your employer has a duty to make your environment safe for you, especially while you are pregnant or if you have given birth in the last six months. If they can't make your job safe because it has inherent hazards, then they have to find you alternative employment for the duration of your pregnancy. This includes reducing over-long hours and changing shifts. If an alternative job is not available, in some cases they will have to offer you paid leave until the risk to you and your baby has passed.

working safely

dangers of workplaces

As soon as you know you are pregnant, or before you plan to be if at all possible, it is wise to sit down and assess your workplace for potential hazards. Your employer will know what these are in the main, but in the end your baby's safety is down to you, so do your own thorough checks too.

Don't forget things peripheral to your job, like excessive noise or smoking, which your employer might overlook. If you are not sure how safe your environment is, consult your doctor or the Health and Safety Executive.

Beyond the actual hazards at work, you should also begin to take more notice of how comfortable your working environment is, such as where you sit, ventilation, heating and allowance for regular breaks. All these things, if not considered, can cause extra tiredness and stress to a pregnant woman.

chemicals

Toxic biological and chemical agents come top of the list of potential hazards. The Advisory Committee on Dangerous Pathogens gives group classifications (see page 74).

physical stress

Exercise, modified to the various stages of pregnancy, is a good thing, but physical stress, such as standing for long hours, lifting or carrying heavy or unwieldy items, climbing to dangerous heights and working underground or in cramped, airless or confined spaces, can be debilitating when your balance, physical strength, endurance and general sensitivity change during pregnancy.

mental stress

You might be set unrealistic targets, have to work long hours and be in an uncomfortably competitive environment. With your emotions awry and your system slowing down to take the baby's needs into account, this sort of job will put undue strain on you.

noise pollution

Don't underestimate the distress caused by the constant loud noise generated by machines, from smaller electric drills and saws to large industrial machinery.

unsociable hours

Working shifts may be tolerable when you have no other pressures in your life but, now you are pregnant, the lack of time to relax could make you tired and ill.

infection

Infection in the workplace is often difficult to avoid. However, if you think that someone may be falling ill, try to avoid them.

restrictive clothing

Some jobs require you to wear protective clothing, which can be stuffy, hot and restrictive. This will be uncomfortable while you are pregnant. Uniforms designed with tight neck, waist or wrist bands and clothes made in synthetic materials can make you itch and sweat as your pregnancy advances.

temperature extremes

Places where it is either uncomfortably hot, such as some factory furnaces and kitchens, or where it is very cold, such as refrigeration plants, can be difficult environments for you during your pregnancy as your temperature control will become much more volatile. (See page 80.)

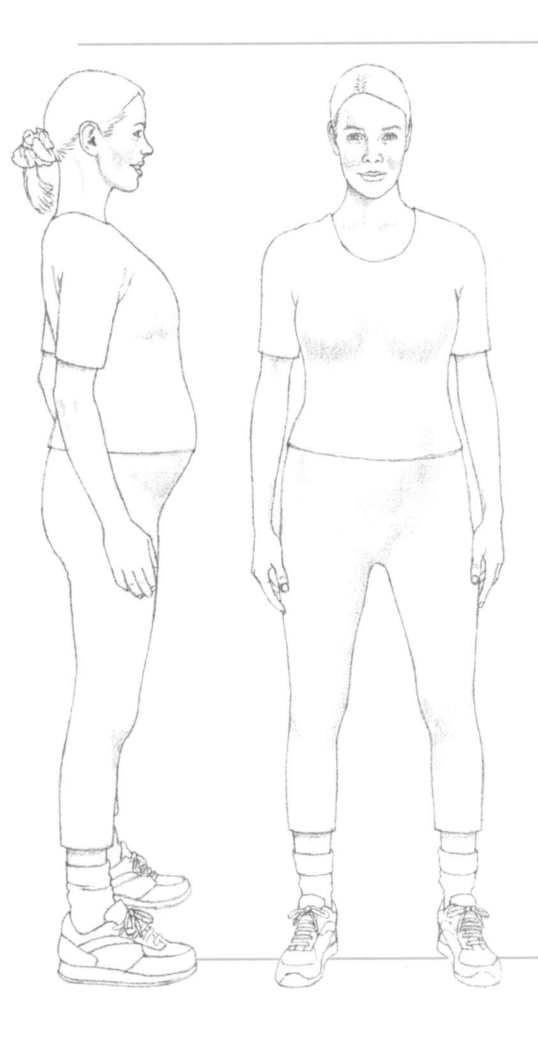

THE IMPORTANCE OF POSTURE

Stretching and exercising the parts of your body that come under particular strain at your workplace is very important when you are pregnant. It is vital to make sure you stand properly if you are to protect your back from strain and injury as the baby pulls your centre of gravity forward and your weight increases.

Stand with your arms relaxed by your sides and your weight evenly distributed on both feet, which should be flat on the floor, a little wider than your hips. Most of us are inclined to either rest on the inside or the outside of our feet without realizing it so keep an eye on this. Lengthen your spine by stretching your torso upwards, taking care not to arch your spine, to give more room under your ribs. Tilt your pelvis forward and tighten your stomach muscles to protect your lower back. Relax your shoulders, look straight ahead and do not lock your knees. When you are standing correctly, your neck and back will be in a straight line.

There are exercises that you can do while you are at work listed in this section. They have been placed with the specific environment that they will be the most helpful for, although they are also useful in a more general way as they will keep you mobile.

offices

The office, on the whole, is not a dangerous environment for you during your pregnancy, but there are still some areas of concern that you should be aware of and, if necessary, adapt to your condition.

display screen equipment

Most office workers spend much of their time in front of a VDU, and there has been considerable anxiety about the safety of this equipment for pregnant women. However, in the UK the National Radiological Protection Board says that the levels of radiation are well below those set in the international recommendations for limiting risk to health and indicates that no protective measures are needed. But, if you are still worried, ask for a protective shield to be fitted to your VDU.

desk comfort

You will need a chair that supports your back and is adjustable to your desk height and VDU. Ask for a foot support so that your feet aren't crossed and scrunched up under your chair. Also, take frequent breaks and move about to allow your circulation to flow freely.

Is your workplace properly ventilated? If it isn't, then make sure you get frequent breaks in the fresh air.

exercises for the office

Being stuck behind a desk all day, or hunched over a telephone or computer, is bad for anyone. However, as your pregnancy advances you will become more aware of muscle aches and pains, so it is a good idea to keep your body mobile to minimize discomfort. Combine the exercises that are listed below and illustrated opposite with your general fitness programme.

breathing Learning how to breathe properly helps your posture and reduces stress and tension in your body. Sit well supported with your shoulders relaxed and your hands resting lightly on the lower curve of your abdomen. Breathe in slowly and deeply, feeling your abdomen gently swell. Hold your breath for a moment then exhale slowly.

arm circles This exercise warms up and loosens your shoulders and also opens up your chest. It is especially good if you have been hunched over your work. Stand with your feet hip-width apart, with your arms relaxed by your sides. Facing forwards, take your right arm around in a slow circle, starting with a forward action, bringing your arm close to your ear and then as far back as possible in a slow continuous motion. Keep your abdominals tight and don't arch your back. Bring your arm back to your side, check your shoulders are relaxed, then repeat the exercise with your left arm. Do eight repetitions with each arm in all.

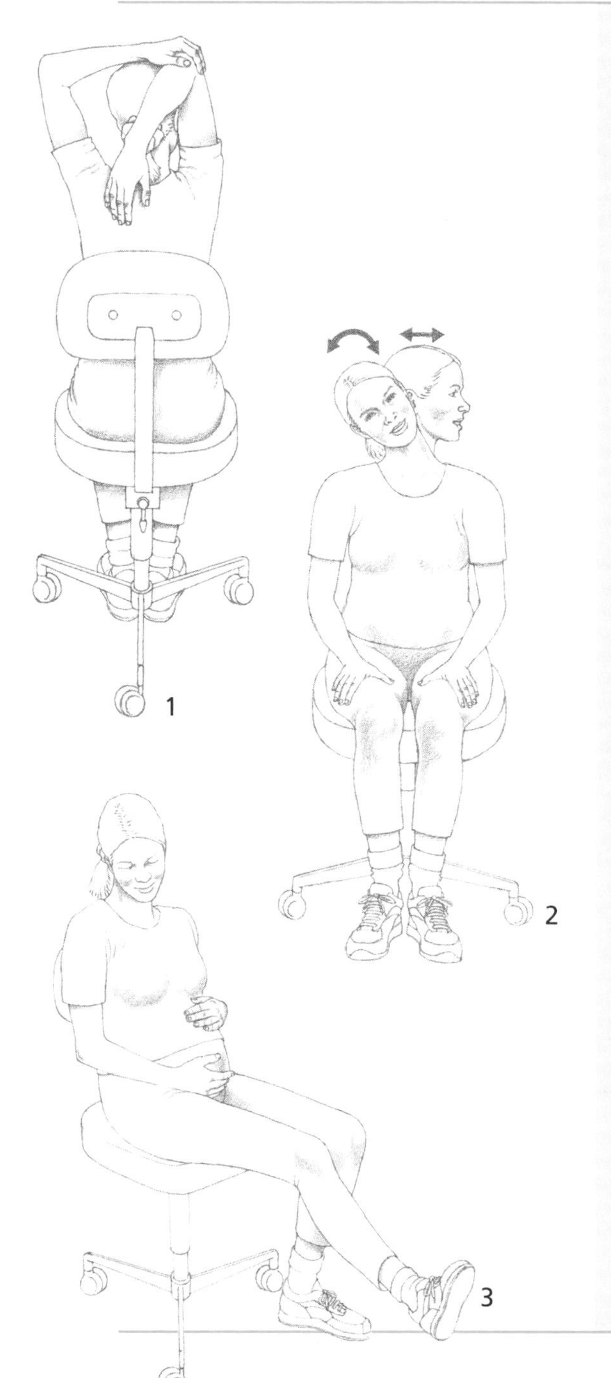

1 SEATED SHOULDER STRETCH

This is an exercise to loosen your shoulder and arm muscles, as well as your neck and back.

- Sitting straight with your feet flat on the floor, slowly stretch your right arm up.
- Bend your elbow, drop your hand down your back, and press your elbow further down with your left hand.
- Hold for 20 seconds and then repeat the process with the other arm.

2 HEAD AND NECK TILTS AND TURNS

Keeping the muscles flexible in your neck and shoulders prevents tension building in your upper body. The two alternatives to this exercise can both be done unobtrusively at your desk.

- Sit up tall, with your shoulders relaxed and your head up straight, then gently tilt your head, bringing your right ear over towards your right shoulder.
- Return to the centre then tilt to the left.
- Repeat this sequence five times.
- Alternatively, sit up straight in your chair and keep your shoulders relaxed. Turn your head slowly to the right, return to the centre, then slowly turn it to the left.
- Repeat this sequence five times. Both exercises can also be combined together.

3 LEG AND ANKLE MOBILIZER

This movement improves circulation, helps to avoid cramp and tones the muscles in your calf and thigh.

- Sitting comfortably in your chair, with your back well supported, lift your right foot a little way off the floor and begin to draw the alphabet in the air with your foot, keeping your left leg still.
- Repeat the process with your left foot, then repeat the whole thing twice more.

laboratory hazards

Working in a laboratory carries many potential risks from biological and chemical agents, depending on what type of work you are engaged in. Some of the agents listed below, although potentially hazardous, may in fact pose no risk if exposure is below a level that might cause harm. Even so, avoid them during pregnancy.

biological agents

Biological agents are categorized and labelled in groups according to the type and degree of hazard they pose to pregnant mothers and their unborn child. The ones to avoid are groups 2,3 and 4. Pregnant women whose work does not actively involve these agents are also vulnerable, but a laboratory worker might be specifically in danger of exposure to them from laboratory specimens. Such agents include hepatitis B, HIV and AIDS, listeria, parvovirus, rubella, TB, syphilis and typhoid.

chemical agents

There are around 200 substances regulated and labelled under an EEC directive that have different risk categories. These include mercury, lead and asbestos. You should also avoid substances that have powerful and nauseating smells.

You need to check the labels on the chemicals you work with to see if they could be potentially hazardous to you and your unborn foetus. The labels contain codings and the chemical agents are listed within the codings. It is important that you check the labels of such substances before you think of becoming pregnant, or as early as possible afterwards. For more information on any of these substances, consult the Control of Substances Hazardous to Health Regulations, (COSHH), which you can obtain through contacting the Health and Safety Executive.

CHEMICAL AGENTS

- R40: Possible risk of irreversible effects.
- R45: May cause cancer.
- R46: May cause heritable genetic damage to the unborn child.
- R61: May cause harm to the unborn child.
- R63: There is a possible risk of harm to the unborn child.
- R64: May cause harm to breastfed babies.

avoiding contamination

To avoid being contaminated, you should adhere to good basic hygiene, which means washing your hands thoroughly and regularly. Also, avoid injuries from needles and sharp objects and wear protective clothing, such as masks, eye shields, latex gloves and clothes that offer proper coverage if necessary. Avoid contact with potentially dangerous substances and vaccinate against potential hazards.

hospitals

Unfortunately, a hospital environment is packed with hazards for the pregnant woman, but all hospitals are regulated by the Control of Substances Hazardous to Health Regulations (COSHH), which you should consult if you are in doubt about the safety of your work environment. Here are some hazards to consider.

x-rays

If you work in the X-ray department of a hospital, or in a dental surgery, you will already have control limits on the amount of external radiation you are exposed to, and will wear a protective apron. Being pregnant, however, must make you extra vigilant. If you suspect a machine is not functioning properly, feel your work colleagues are casual about risk or your protective clothing is old and worn out, ask for changes to be made.

As you get larger, the protective apron will be more uncomfortable, but you should still make sure it covers your abdomen adequately. *Ionizing Radiations Regulations*, 1985 will tell you the statutory dose limits for pregnant women (available from the Health and Safety Executive).

drugs

Most drugs you may come into contact with will not damage you or your baby, with the exception of cytotoxic drugs – the drugs used to combat cancer, which may cause damage to genetic information in sperm and eggs. You could absorb the toxins through your skin or through inhalation. Pharmacists, nurses and doctors are at risk through handling or administration of these drugs. Avoid needle injuries, dispose of waste carefully, wear protective clothing and keep exposure to these drugs at an absolute minimum.

lifting

Nurses in particular will need to be careful about lifting during pregnancy. Although lifting techniques will minimize damage to your back, lifting another human being is unpredictable, tiring and potentially hazardous so try to avoid doing so while pregnant.

handling specimens

Nurses, doctors and laboratory technicians in hospitals are constantly called upon to take specimens of blood, urine and other body fluids. Wear protective clothing such as glasses, masks and gloves and pay particular attention to storage and waste disposal.

infections

Hospital workers are in the front line of exposure to infections. Your employer should have infection control policies with specific references to the risks to pregnant women.

classrooms

A school can be quite a stressful environment for a pregnant woman. There is a lot of noise, children rushing about pushing and shoving and a constant demand on your attention. Depending on the subjects you teach, there are also particular hazards, such as those associated with sport, to be considered. Travelling home while carrying heavy loads of homework can also be difficult.

standing too long

You will find standing increasingly tiring as your pregnancy advances, so minimize it as much as possible. Ask for a high stool you can perch on at the blackboard, do the exercises shown opposite and sit as often as you can.

get the children's support

Explain to your class that you are pregnant and that it might be dangerous to your baby if you are bumped and pushed too hard.

Your pregnancy can actually be a great opportunity for involving the children in a learning process as it progresses; it will be something they might all find interesting.

mental stress

Teachers suffer from high stress levels, which is not good for your baby. If you find your job mentally stressful, you should minimize extra commitments and consider taking your maternity leave as soon as you can.

sport

If you teach sport, avoid very strenuous exercise, especially in the first months when you are still at risk of a miscarriage. Do not engage in gymnastic exercises that require balance or might strain your ligaments. Don't allow yourself to get too out of breath and always take proper breaks. Finally, avoid games where you might be hit by balls.

infection risk

In schools, the risk of diseases being passed from person to person is high. As a teacher you will be in contact with fevers and many infectious diseases, although most of these are rare in adults due to immunization. But don't hesitate to send a child home who has a high fever while you are pregnant.

avoiding confrontation

Keeping the attention of a large class of potentially unruly teenagers can be a problem for anyone, and even smaller children can be very challenging and difficult at times. But you should try to avoid any confrontation that could lead to aggression and might carry both physical and emotional consequences. If you feel you are in any danger of being attacked, walk away and get help from your colleagues.

1 WALL STRETCHING

This simple exercise is useful for lifting your ribs off your pelvis when your baby gets bigger.

- Sit with your back pressed firmly against a wall. First raise one arm outwards and upwards against the wall until it is just above head height. Then raise the other in a similar way to join it.
- Sit like this, arms raised, for as long as you like.

2 SIDE STRETCH

This exercise lengthens your spine and stretches the upper back muscles to counteract stiff shoulders and a weak back.

- Relax your shoulders and, with your feet wider than your hips and your knees not locked, place your hands on your hips. Keeping your stomach muscles tight, tilt your pelvis slightly forward.
- Stretch your right arm upwards just in front of your head and reach up towards the ceiling.
- Bend directly to the left, reaching your arm up and over your head.
- Hold for a count of five, then do the other side.

3 CALF STRETCH

This is useful if you suffer from cramp from standing too long in one position.

- Stand with your right side to a chair and place your hand on the back for support.
- Tighten your abdominals and, with your feet about hip-width apart and pointing forwards, take a step backwards with your left foot.
- Keep your knees soft and lengthen your spine.
- Bend your right leg and straighten your left one, pressing your left heel into the floor.
- Keep your weight forward and pelvis tilted slightly forward. Move your foot further back if the stretch is not noticeable.
- Hold for a count of 10 and then swap and do the stretch on the other side.

manual work

Manual work is the sort of activity that you might do in a factory or in the retail trade. It does not involve heavy physical strain, but sometimes the environment will nevertheless be uncomfortable for a pregnant woman. Make sure you get proper breaks each day, whatever your job, during which you can eat, do some gentle exercise and get some fresh air.

using chemicals

If you are working where chemicals are used, such as glue, dry-cleaning materials, hairdressing products, petrol, paint-strippers and thinners, creosote, lead or mercury, then check their potential toxicity and take action to avoid even minimal exposure (see page 74).

noise and vibrations

Noise can be a problem in some factories where heavy machinery is used. Your job may not involve danger from the machinery itself, but you might still be subjected to unreasonable levels of noise. Whereas this will not specifically put your baby at risk, it causes strain that may lead to tiredness and raised blood pressure. If you work in an environment where noise levels are very high, you should ask to be moved to a quieter area during your pregnancy. Consult the *Noise at Work Regulations*, 1989 for details (available from the Health and Safety Executive).

Some research suggests that vibrations caused by driving or riding in off-road vehicles or working heavy machinery might lead to miscarriage. If you're concerned, avoid this.

dangerous machinery

If you are operating machinery that puts you in danger of injury, or your particular field of work means you are working in an uncomfortably confined space, then ask to be moved to another job during your pregnancy. If this isn't possible then you might be eligible for paid leave for the months until your maternity leave begins.

lifting and handling

Lifting anything other than light, manageable objects is not advisable while you are pregnant. Not only are you more susceptible to injury from your weakened ligaments, but your balance becomes uncertain and your back vulnerable. Even if the objects are light, you should take care to lift correctly (see opposite). Avoid standing on ladders to reach things or excessive reaching to high places from the ground, where your balance might be compromised. Carrying large, unwieldy objects, even if they are not heavy, also threatens your balance. And, if you have had a caesarean section you must avoid heavy lifting for the first three months after the birth.

useful exercises

If you work in a factory or some sort of retail environment, the exercises detailed here and below will be useful for you.

shoulder roll This is for reducing tension and aching in your upper back from carrying loads as well as from general poor posture. Sit on a chair with your back well-supported, shoulders relaxed, head straight. Put your fingers on your shoulders and rotate your elbows back and round in a circle. Do this for five circles, then rotate in the opposite direction. Repeat as often as you like.

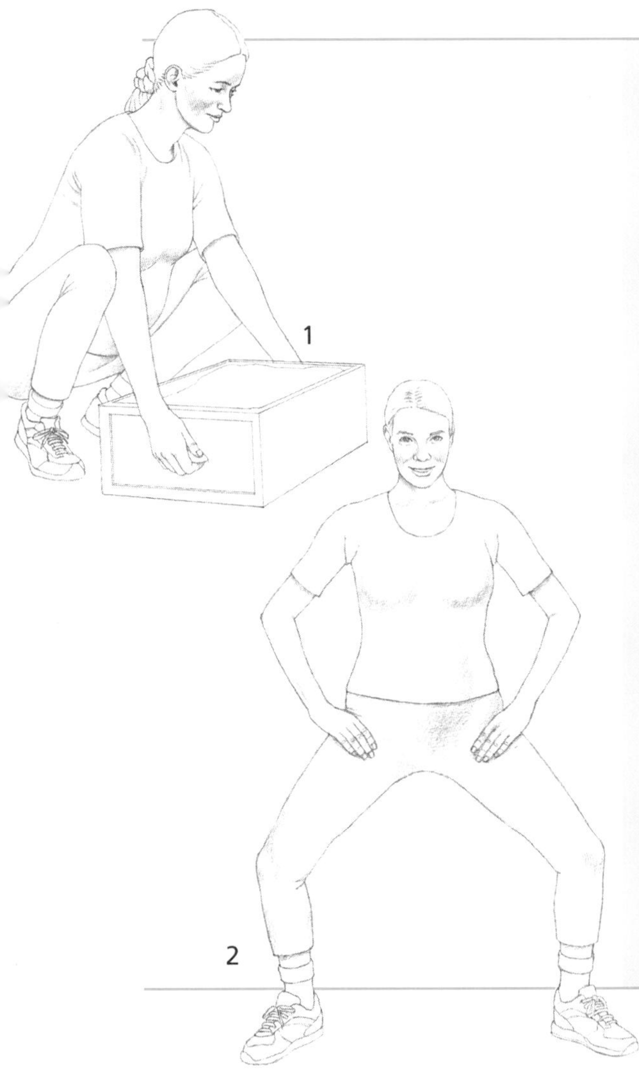

1 LIFTING

Only lift light, easily accessible objects.

- Squat down to the level of the object, with your knees bent, legs apart and feet on the floor, in order to give you a solid base to lift from.
- Grasp the object to be lifted with both hands and hold it close to your body. When you have a firm grip, and not before, slowly stand up.
- Do not lift an object at arms' length.
- Do not lift when standing or balancing on anything but a firm, non-slippery surface.

2 KNEE BEND

Practise this exercise to strengthen and mobilize your knees and thighs to help with carrying the extra weight of your baby. (It can also be helpful if you want to squat during labour.)

- With your feet turned out a little and wider than your hips, place your hands on your hips and straighten your spine.
- Tighten your stomach muscles and tilt your pelvis forward a little.
- Slowly bend your knees, keeping your back straight and head up. Don't go too low, only as far as is comfortable.
- Keeping your stomach firm, slowly return to the upright position, keeping your knees unlocked. Repeat the whole process five times.

restaurants and cafés

Whether you are part of the waiting staff or work in the kitchen, restaurants and cafés have a number of problems for pregnant women. This is because they can be crowded, noisy, smoky and frantic at peak times, and the hours are often long and unsocial. Here are some of the difficulties you will need to overcome.

long hours

The nature of the restaurant business requires employees to work long hours. Although this is not specifically dangerous to you or your baby, you will find these hours increasingly tiring as your pregnancy progresses. As most places operate a shift system, ask to work daylight hours, and make sure you get proper breaks during your shift.

carrying

If you are waiting tables, your job will involve carrying loads back and forth from kitchen to table. As speed is often an issue it is easy to attempt to carry too much but while you are pregnant you will have to be realistic about how much you can safely carry. Lift correctly (see page 79) and beware of heavy swinging doors, which might hit your stomach.

standing

Whether in the kitchen or the serving area, you will be on your feet for most of your shift. To avoid leg swelling and varicose veins, wear support tights if your legs are aching, as well as sensible, flat shoes that give you proper support. Avoid socks with restricting tops.

smoky atmosphere

Although most restaurants now enforce no-smoking areas, there are plenty that do not. It is not wise to spend long hours in such an atmosphere so, if your job requires you to do so, find out if there is an alternative. Passive smoking is not as bad as actually smoking yourself, but a quantity of nicotine will still reach your baby.

heat

When you are pregnant, you will be less able to tolerate the heat, and will be susceptible to fainting, excessive sweating and heat stress. If you work in a kitchen that is hot, you might have to find alternative work in a different area. Make sure there is somewhere for you to sit if you feel overcome at any time and drink plenty of filtered water during the day.

smells

You will be sensitive, especially in the early months, to strong smells and may feel nauseous. Much of the nausea in pregnancy is due to low blood sugar, so don't go to work on an empty stomach and keep a supply of crackers to nibble on if you do feel sick.

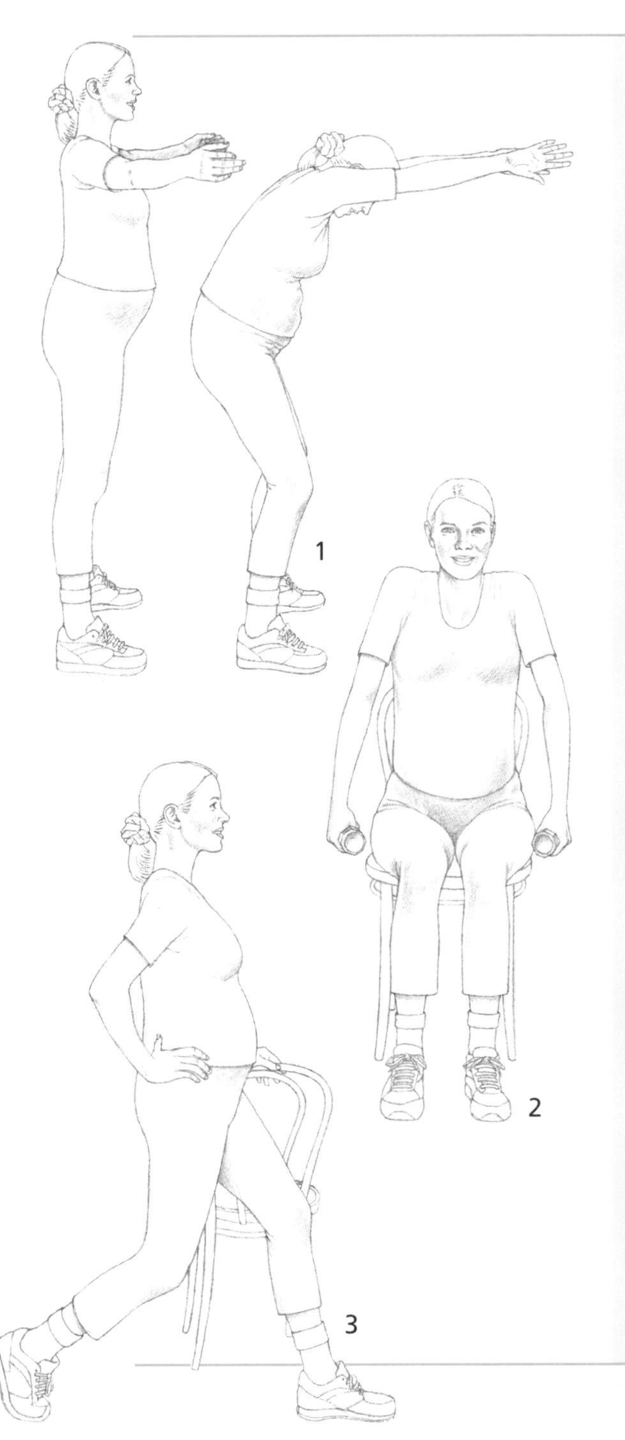

1 CHEST OPENER

This releases and stretches your upper body.

- Stand tall, feet a little wider than your body, your arms loose by your sides. Tilt your pelvis slightly forward and keep your stomach firm. Bring both arms up, level with your shoulders.
- Slowly curl forwards, rounding your back and bringing your arms together in front of you.
- Keeping your arms level with your shoulders, bring them back out to the side, straightening your spine and pulling your shoulders down.
- Repeat this five times.

2 SITTING SHOULDER SHRUG

This is a good exercise for strengthening the upper back muscles for lifting and carrying, and can be done using small weights.

- Sit upright in a straight-backed chair, your back well-supported with a cushion if necessary.
- Relax your shoulders while holding a weight in each hand, keeping your hands by your sides. Sit tall and tighten your abdominals.
- Lift your shoulders up towards your ears as if shrugging. Hold this position for a moment, then lower your shoulders. Don't lock your elbows.
- Do three sets of five repetitions.

3 HIP STRETCH

This strengthens the muscles that support your hips, which is important when you are standing all day and carrying the weight of your baby.

- Stand beside an upright chair, with your left hand on it as shown. Starting with your feet forwards and a little wider than your hips, step back with your right foot, and keep its heel off the floor. Keep your weight evenly distributed, stomach muscles tight and lengthen your spine.
- Bend both knees at the same time and tilt your pelvis forward, with your bottom tucked under, until you feel a stretch in your left thigh. Hold for a count of five, then repeat with the other leg.

agriculture

Agricultural work tends to be physically demanding, and also exposes the worker to chemicals and infections that might affect the health and welfare of an unborn baby. Special care has to be taken on all these counts during pregnancy, as well as during the period of planning and conception.

physical strain

Be careful of physically overdoing things, especially in the first months when the risk of having a miscarriage is at its highest. You will become tired much more easily, but also risk straining your muscles as your pregnancy hormones weaken your ligaments.

vibrations

Driving a tractor or riding in an off-road vehicle, which can expose you to the risk of violent bumps, excessive movement and vibrations, is best avoided.

lifting

We have dealt with lifting on pages 78–80, and stated that heavy lifting is not advised at any stage in pregnancy, but be particularly careful if you are handling animals that might struggle and kick. This is also true for women who have recently had a caesarean section.

chemicals

Many agricultural workers are in potential danger of exposure to chemicals such as pesticides and sheep dip. The toxicity can be absorbed either through contact splashes to the skin or through inhalation of vapour. *The Control of Pesticides Regulations*, 1986 marks hazardous substances 'Sk'. Check the labelling on all products and wear protective clothing such as eye shields, gloves, overalls and rubber boots if you are exposed to such substances. Avoid them during pregnancy.

infections

There are two potentially dangerous infections that are particularly related to contact with animals. Page 25 has further details, but below are risks specific to agricultural work.

toxoplasmosis Animal faeces should always be considered at risk of transmitting infection.

chlamydia This infection can be caught from sheep at lambing time. Therefore, avoid all direct contact with ewes, newborn lambs and their placentas while pregnant. If you absolutely have to handle sheep at lambing time, make sure you pay strict attention to hand washing and wear protective gloves. Also be careful when handling clothing that may have been contaminated.

horticulture

Workers in the horticultural industry run many of the same risks as those in agriculture do. However, one of the problems that is specific to this area is the amount of time that horticulturists have to spend bending over, which can cause severe backache.

You must be particularly careful of your back when you are pregnant, as you are carrying extra weight and your balance is compromised. Don't forget that your muscles and ligaments are weakened by the pregnancy hormones flooding your body.

Whenever possible, kneel down on a padded kneeler and place yourself close to the area you are working so you do not pull muscles from stretching. And do not stand on ladders or branches to reach plants.

infection

Soil contamination, from chemicals such as pesticide sprays and fertilizers or toxoplasma infection, is a hazard for anyone working on the land. Cat faeces, which carry diseases, are also present in many gardens. Wearing gloves when gardening is a good precaution, but also beware of hand-to-mouth infection after handling garden equipment or plants that are soil-covered. Wash your hands thoroughly after any contact.

using garden equipment

Digging, hoeing, pruning and mowing all involve working with potentially dangerous tools. Make sure you treat these implements with particular care to avoid injuries when pregnant. Working on trees, with possible injury from falling branches, or with powerful sawing equipment should be avoided.

If your job involves garden reconstruction, such as laying paving stones, building trellis and fences or excavation work, do not be tempted to move or lift large objects or do any heavy digging. All these can result in miscarriage or serious muscle injury.

physical labour

Gardening is hard, physical work so make sure that you take plenty of breaks, so that you don't get overtired. If you are working in strong sunlight, protect yourself from the possibility of heat exhaustion, as you will be much more vulnerable to it while you are pregnant. Cover up, wear a hat and spend lots of time in the shade.

You should also be aware that working in an overheated greenhouse could expose you to the possibility of fainting and heat stress. Drink plenty of water when doing any such physical work, but try to avoid major physical strain during your pregnancy.

the travel industry

Travelling in itself has not been shown to endanger a pregnant woman or her baby at all, and it is even possible to fly until the last few weeks before your baby's birth. However, it is best to avoid travelling abroad in the first weeks, until blood tests and ultrasounds confirm your pregnancy is on course.

Don't forget that the first three months carry the risk of early miscarriage or the possibility of an ectopic (tubal) pregnancy and, while many countries have excellent medical facilities, some others do not. And even if there are good medical facilities, you might still have to deal with a potentially traumatic situation without your familiar network of support around you if you are stranded in a foreign country.

motion sickness

Especially in the early months of pregnancy, women are prone to motion sickness, which can be exacerbated by many things, including the motion of a road vehicle or boat, or turbulence in a plane. To avoid or alleviate it, never allow yourself to go for long periods without eating and drinking, eat small meals regularly and carry glucose sweets and dry crackers to ward off the first pangs of hunger. Avoid caffeine and alcohol while travelling and remember to drink plenty of water if you are being sick, to replace lost fluids. Ginger biscuits, ginger tea or ginger capsules are said to help in some cases, as is the Bach Flower Remedy, Rescue Remedy.

infection risk

Beware of eating in situations abroad where food hygiene is poor, such as roadside stalls or beach cafés. It is easy to pick up salmonella, e-coli or listeria from dirty, poorly cooked, poorly stored or unpasteurized food (see page 25 for further details of these diseases). Always wash your hands thoroughly, avoid salads where the vegetables might have been washed in contaminated water and eat fruit that you can peel. Ice cubes and ice-cream also pose risks from impure water.

If you do get ill, don't be tempted to resort to medication, just drink plenty of bottled water. If your symptoms persist or you are worried about their severity, consult a doctor sooner rather than later, and immediately explain that you are pregnant.

Coming into constant close contact with a lot of people in a confined space, such as on a coach or plane, will inevitably increase your chances of catching any passing viruses or bacteria. If you think one of your passengers has a fever, make sure you give them a wide berth and ask a colleague to explain to them why it is necessary for you to do so.

immunizations

It is always important to keep your immunizations up to date, but some vaccinations cause possible risk to the baby if they are given while you are pregnant. If you have been exposed to an infection, you and your doctor need to decide whether the risk of vaccination is greater than the consequences of contracting the disease. Only take anti-malarial pills while pregnant after discussion with a specialist in this field. Be sure to consult your doctor if planning to travel to an area where malaria is prevalent.

jet lag

If you work in the airline industry, flying long hours to different time zones can play havoc with your body clock. You will find you are much less able to cope with this disruption while you are pregnant, and you risk getting overtired. Ask your employer if you can change to shorter flights or work on the ground during your pregnancy.

risky sports

If your job involves supervising sport and activities for holiday makers, avoid any sort of diving or dangerous sports such as water-skiing or sky-diving while pregnant.

Diving using compressed air, or working in pressurized enclosures, could seriously harm your baby. This is because of the risk of developing the bends, when bubbles of gas enter the maternal circulation. Therefore, you must not dive or work in compressed air if you are pregnant.

far from home

If you are still travelling in the later weeks of your pregnancy, remember that you are putting yourself at risk of giving birth away from your support network and the facilities you have chosen and are familiar with. It is best to stay within 45 minutes of home and hospital in the final weeks.

sunburn

Working in a hot country inevitably exposes you to the sun. You will be less able to tolerate extremes of temperature and will be more susceptible to fainting, excessive sweating and heat stress. Therefore, while you are pregnant try to stay in the shade wherever possible and, if you have to be out in the sun for a short period, cover up with hat, glasses and a T-shirt. Remember to drink plenty of water at all times in order to avoid getting dehydrated.

uniform

Ensure that your uniform fits properly and is not restrictive. If you have to wear a uniform, such as a cabin crew's outfit, then you will need to order a larger size in advance to accommodate your pregnancy. And remember to wear comfortable, low-heeled shoes.

> Whatever industry you are working in, make sure that you inform your employers as soon as possible about your pregnancy, so that provision can be made for you and your baby's comfort and safety.

maternity legislation

Your employer should be aware of his or her legal commitments to pregnant women in the workforce, obligations that are enshrined in law. It is important that you know your rights, and what you are entitled to contractually, ie the specific rights that your company offers to women taking maternity leave, such as extra maternity pay. As soon as you are pregnant, check your contract if you are uncertain about your company policy, or talk to your personnel department or union.

Up until you begin your maternity leave, your rights centre around taking reasonable time off for antenatal appointments and classes and are not connected to how long you have been in your job, but there are various different categories of maternity benefits after you finish work. These depend on how long you have worked for your employer when you become pregnant, how much you earn and specific contractual benefits. Make sure that you understand what your options are before you make any decisions about your future.

There are also unforeseen circumstances that are easier to deal with when you know your rights, such as illness, changing your mind about returning to work, the decision to continue breastfeeding after you return and unfair dismissal. Don't leave it to others to tell you your entitlements; they may get their facts wrong or be manipulating your situation to their advantage. If you need more advice, contact the Maternity Alliance, who publish leaflets on maternity rights and benefits. Unfortunately many maternity rights only apply to employees, not to contract workers (eg agency temps and casuals) and the self-employed. If you fall into one of these categories, it is best to contact the Maternity Alliance and Citizens Advice Bureau for further information.

your rights

You will be given a maternity certificate called a MAT B1 by your doctor or midwife when you are about six months pregnant. You do not legally have to tell your employer that you are pregnant until 21 days before your leave begins but it is often best to do this as soon as you can. Your entitlements are explained here.

You cannot start your leave until 11 weeks before the week in which your due date falls, which is around your 29th week of pregnancy. (To calculate this, count back 11 Sundays from the Sunday before your EDD. So, for example, if your EDD is 1 June 2001, your maternity leave can start on 11 March, and you must tell your employer by 18 February.) However, most employers prefer to have as much notice as possible, so that a suitable replacement can be found. You decide when you want to begin your leave, not your employer, and you may carry on up until the birth, subject to pregnancy-related illness. Put your maternity leave notice in writing, not just verbally, and have a copy of your MAT B1 handy in case your employer asks for it. Include your EDD, the date you wish to start your leave and a request for Statutory Maternity Pay (SMP) in your notice. You do not have to state whether you intend to return to work at this stage.

statutory maternity pay

You will be paid SMP if you have worked for the same employer for at least 26 weeks by the end of the qualifying week, which is the 15th week before the week in which your EDD falls and around the 26th week of pregnancy. (Find the Sunday before your baby is due and count back 15 Sundays.) To qualify you must earn an average of at least £67 per week, before tax, in the eight weeks (if paid weekly) or two months (if paid monthly) before the end of the qualifying week, and still be employed in the qualifying week.

SMP is paid for 18 weeks from when you start maternity leave and is paid at 90 per cent of your average pay for the first six weeks, calculated on the amount you received in the eight weeks/two months up to the last pay day before the end of the qualifying week. For the remaining 12 weeks SMP is given at the flat rate of £60.20 per week and is paid in the same way as your normal salary, with the same deductions.

You are entitled to this benefit regardless of your commitment to return to work, and if you do not return you do not have to pay back any of the SMP you have received.

maternity allowance

If you have not been in continuous employment throughout your pregnancy, you have changed jobs while pregnant or are self-employed, and are therefore not entitled to

SMP, you might be eligible for either standard-rate Maternity Allowance or variable-rate Maternity Allowance. You can get MA if you have worked for at least 26 weeks of the 66 immediately before the week your baby is due. Standard rate will be given if you earned at least £67 a week on average in 13 weeks (they do not have to be consecutive.) SRMA is £60.20 for 18 weeks. Variable rate will be given to you if you earn an average of £30 or more a week in 13 consecutive weeks. VRMA is 90 per cent of your average earnings, or £60.20 (whichever is the lesser) for 18 weeks. If in doubt, check with your Benefits Agency. (All figures cited are valid for 2000-01 and change in April each year.)

maternity leave

Ordinary Maternity Leave (OML) is the entitlement to 18 weeks' leave, starting from 11 weeks before the week the baby is due, for any woman employed while she is pregnant, no matter how many hours she has worked or how long she has been in her job, with the right to return to the same job after maternity leave. A woman does not have to give notice of the date she intends to return unless it is earlier than 18 weeks from the day she left on leave.

If you decide that you want to return earlier, you should give your employer 21 days' notice of your intention, but you cannot go back until the Compulsory Maternity Leave is over, which lasts for two weeks after the birth of your baby. During OML you will be paid according to your entitlement to SMP.

additional maternity leave

This is extra time off, usually unpaid unless there are specific contractual benefits, for women who have been in the same job for at least one year and 11 weeks by the week their baby is due. Additional maternity leave (AML) means you can delay your return to work for 29 weeks from the week your baby is actually born. As with OML, you do not need to give notice of your date of return unless it is different from the 29-week deadline. However, your employer can write asking you to confirm your baby's date of birth and whether you intend to return to work any time after the 15th week of your leave. The letter must include information to help you work out when your AML will end and state that you must reply within 21 days. If you don't respond to the letter with the confirmation requested within 21 days you may weaken your protection against unfair dismissal. You are allowed to change your mind later on if you decide to leave work.

When you return after AML you must be offered the same job back, unless that is not reasonably practical. There may, for example, have been a reorganization, in which case you must be offered a suitable job on similar terms and conditions. You can also ask to work shorter hours, part time or request a job share if you prefer not to continue your previous job. Your employer is legally required to consider your request, and must have a business-related reason for refusing. If they can prove that there is a reason for refusal, they may be justified in turning you down.

company policies

A recent survey states that there were 11.8 million women in employment in the UK during 1999. Forty per cent of these had children that were under the age of 18. The average age of women having their first baby is now 26.9, so many are already established in work when they decide to start a family.

Because of the increase in working mothers companies are having to review their labour policies to accommodate the increasing proportion of their workforce who will require maternity considerations. Despite the statutory requirements, companies vary widely in the benefits that they offer to pregnant women and those with families. Some only provide the basic minimum but others have enhanced the requirements and give either better paid, or longer paid, leave.

ANTENATAL CARE

Antenatal care consists of appointments with a registered doctor or midwife concerning your pregnancy. Whatever your company's policies are, as an employee you have a statutory right to reasonable time off for antenatal care, paid at the normal rate, no matter how long you have worked there. (As a part-time or shift worker you may be asked to arrange your appointments outside your working day, but if this is not possible, your employer should still give you time off.) Some employers baulk at relaxation classes, but the government includes these in your antenatal care provided the appointment is made on the advice of a registered doctor, midwife or health visitor.

When you apply for a job, checking the company policy on maternity benefits is probably the last thing on your mind. But it is worth knowing what is being offered by other companies in order to know whether you are being treated with fairness. Unless any shortfall is pointed out to employers, changes will be slow in coming, but with more companies realizing how much they rely on the female workforce, management need to be open to reviewing their policy if necessary.

enhancing statutory benefits

Companies sometimes enhance their statutory benefits to encourage the female workforce to return to work after maternity leave has ended. The enhanced offer is usually paid in a lump sum after the employee's return. Companies that choose to enhance the statutory maternity provisions usually do so by extending the paid maternity leave period (this usually varies depending on the length of service with the company). An employer might top up the Statutory Maternity Pay to full pay instead of 90 per cent for all or part of the first six weeks, top up the lower-paid 12-week period to half pay, offer full pay for the entire 18 weeks or extend the actual period of paid leave. This can be up to 52 weeks in some cases, or six months' paid leave with a further 12 months unpaid. The take-up rate of maternity leave varies according to how much of the leave is paid.

parental leave

This leave is a new right that has been in place in Britain since 15 December 1999. It allows unpaid leave of 13 weeks per parent (not just the mother), per child for all children born after 15 December 1999. You must have been employed for at least a year, and must take the leave by the time the child is five, within five years of a child's placement for adoption or, in the case of a child entitled to disability living allowance, before the child is 18. However, you can only take the leave at a rate of four weeks per year. You must also give a minimum of 21 days' notice to your employer if you wish to take it up.

Some companies have enhanced this scheme for their workforce, as long as proper notice is given, by removing the rule (currently being challenged in the courts as contravening the EU Parenting Leave Directive) limiting the eligibility requirement to those born after 15 December 1999. Some do this by extending the maximum age of the children who are covered by this right, others by allowing their workforce to take more than four weeks in any one year or by being more flexible about leave and notice requirements. Some also give paid parental leave. Ask if your employer has a parental leave scheme, as it may be better than the legal minimum.

BALANCING THE WORKFORCE

More and more companies are responding to the needs of their female workforce and are making it easier for women to return to work after they have had a child. They have made it possible for women to combine an existing family with a career by implementing longer maternity leave, reduced hours schemes, more flexible ways of working and financial incentives for women returning to work.
As flexible working is becoming increasingly commonplace, employers are better able to see the advantages and it is now much more widespread. Some employers have a negative view of such schemes and lean towards employing so-called 'straightforward males', but they are laying themselves open to a charge of unlawful sex discrimination. Further advice on such a situation is available from the Equal Opportunities Commission.

But the root of the problem is not the perfectly reasonable demands that women are at last beginning to make in relation to childcare provision, but the fact that we still see women as the main carers of the family. Paid paternity leave is a far-off ideal in most companies and men are rarely expected to bear an equal responsibility for their children's day-to-day welfare. Men are also still frequently paid more than women to do the same job, which reinforces the male consciousness that their jobs are more important than their partner's.

To achieve a proper recruitment balance in the future, for companies and those they employ, both men and women will have to be allowed more real choices about how they combine their commitment to their family with their careers.

extra legal considerations

Your company should have a staff handbook in which the legal position with regard to unforeseen problems connected to pregnancy and your return to work should be clearly delineated. Have you read it? If not, should a situation occur where your job or contractual rights are threatened in some way, you could be denying yourself your right to benefits or compensation.

job change

It is against the law for an employer to discriminate against you on any account connected with your pregnancy, childbirth or maternity leave. But what happens if you go back at the end of your maternity leave to discover that you are being offered a different job, with a lower salary, a change in location and less status, or your old job is being done by someone else?

Your first step is to talk to your employer and say that you are unhappy with your new job. If you start the new job, make sure that you put in writing that you are only doing so under protest. If you have a union, talk to the representative about your position. If you and your employer are not able to resolve your differences, you may have a claim for sex discrimination and unfair dismissal in an Employment Tribunal. You should make sure that your claim is put forward within three months of returning to work.

However, this is a very complicated area of the law and you should seek further advice from the Citizens Advice Bureau, Maternity Alliance or a Law Centre who will be able to advise you on the up-to-date details.

redundancy

If your employer chooses you for redundancy because you are pregnant or have taken maternity leave, then you may have a claim for unfair dismissal and sex discrimination. However, if you are made redundant lawfully during maternity leave, you are entitled to be given first refusal of any suitable alternative vacancies that exist if they are on similar terms to your previous job. You also take precedence over other workers being made redundant. If your employer fails to offer you any suitable vacancies, you could have a claim for unfair dismissal.

contractual rights

The Employment Rights Act of 1996 states that you retain all of your normal rights, apart from basic salary, during the 18-week period of Ordinary Maternity Leave. For instance, you still have the same holiday entitlement and the same rules about how much and when you take your holiday continue to apply. You should also retain benefits such as luncheon vouchers, health insurance, club membership and subsidized travel and should also be allowed to keep the company car if you have one. After the 18 weeks of OML, however, if you are also taking Additional Maternity Leave, you continue to be an employee – but are not entitled to your usual terms and conditions unless they are offered by your employer. The only terms that continue during AML are the right to paid notice, redundancy pay, grievance and disciplinary procedures, duty of trust and confidence and to act in good faith.

pay review and promotion You are entitled to any annual pay rise that you would normally receive in the terms of your contract, and should also be considered for promotion if it arises when you are on your leave. Your employer should inform you of any interviews for such a promotional post, and ensure that you are given a fair chance to attend them if you wish to.

holidays and normal pay You continue to accrue your statutory right to 20 days' paid holiday a year throughout maternity leave (OML and AML). Additional contractual holiday continues to accrue during OML, but does not accrue during AML.

You cannot claim normal pay, but you may qualify for maternity pay during OML.

application to a tribunal

Suppose you and your employer still cannot agree about a grievance, and you feel you are being unfairly discriminated against because of your pregnancy. Your employer may not be familiar with the legal obligations regarding pregnant workers, so it may be worth obtaining the relevant factsheet from the Maternity Alliance for them to read. If this doesn't work and you feel you have to resort to an Employment Tribunal, here are some of the things you should know about the process:

- You must make the claim within three months of the date of the dismissal or discrimination. There needs to be a very good reason for applying late and it isn't worth the risk so make sure you do it promptly.
- It often takes a long time, six months or more, before your claim comes before the Tribunal. You may win and get compensation, but you may not, so don't rush into resignation on the supposition that you will win, otherwise you might face unemployment without any compensation. Get legal advice before you resign.
- A sex discrimination claim rests on you being unfairly treated because of your pregnancy or maternity leave. If you have been sacked you will be able to claim for unfair dismissal as well.
- You will need form IT1, which is available from your Citizens Advice Bureau, to make an Employment Tribunal claim. You will not be liable for your employer's costs and there is no cost to start the claim. You may be able to get a lawyer to take your case on a 'no win, no fee' basis, which means that their fee is paid out of any compensation that you win. Make sure that you understand all the legal and financial implications of going to an Employment Tribunal before embarking on the process, as it can be very drawn out and stressful in some cases.

pensions and supplementary benefits

Retirement seems a long way off when you are starting a family and it is easy to go along with the company pension scheme. But if you are considering one or more periods of maternity leave or a career break, it is worth checking to make sure your pension suits your life plan. (Rates listed here were correct for 2000-01.)

money purchase pension

This pension includes personal pensions and it is the kind that you and/or your employer contribute to. It consists of a percentage of your salary. Your pension payout will depend on how much has been contributed in total.

If it is your employer who contributes to your pension, then the normal amount must continue to be paid during your 18 weeks of paid maternity leave and during any contractual maternity pay, even if your maternity pay is lower than your usual salary.

If you are paying your contributions yourself, your payments will be based on the maternity pay you are receiving, not your normal pay. You may be able to make up any shortfall with extra contributions when you return to work. If you have more complex arrangements, you should consult a pension adviser for further information.

final salary pension

This pension is based on the length of time you have worked for your employer and the amount you are earning when you leave. When you are away on paid maternity leave, which includes Statutory Maternity Pay and any contractual maternity pay, you are still considered to be on pensionable service, your continuity of employment is not affected and your final benefit entitlement remains the same as it would be had you not been absent. If you take unpaid leave you are not considered to be on pensionable service, but your continuity of employment for pension purposes remains intact. So your pensionable service period begins before your period of unpaid leave and continues after you return.

state retirement pension

To make certain that your National Insurance contribution record is intact so that you qualify for the State Retirement Pension, make sure that you contact the National Insurance Contributions Office to have credits awarded for the time when you are being paid the lower rate of SMP. If you are receiving Maternity Allowance or Incapacity Benefit (see page 95), you will automatically receive these credits for each week that you are on the benefit.

tax and national insurance

You pay tax and National Insurance on your higher rate of Statutory Maternity Pay, (90 per cent of your earnings for the first six weeks) and it will have been deducted at source. However, the lower rate that you receive for the next 12 weeks is below the tax and National Insurance level so no contributions are required.

incapacity benefit

This is for pregnant women who do not qualify for SMP or Maternity Allowance, but who have paid some National Insurance Contributions during the previous two tax years, although not in the current one. You will be paid £50.90 per week for six weeks before your baby is born and for two weeks after. You should contact your local Benefits Agency to find out whether you are eligible for this. It is worth making a claim because entitlement is not a straightforward issue.

benefits for low income

If you are being paid Income Support, job-seekers or working families tax credit, you can claim a Sure Start Maternity Grant of £300 to help you buy things for your baby. You should therefore inform your social security office as soon as you know you are pregnant. You might also qualify for free milk and vitamins and financial help with fares to and from the hospital for your antenatal appointments.

registering your baby

You are legally required to register your baby within six weeks of her birth in England, Wales and Northern Ireland, and within three weeks in Scotland. To do this, go to your local registry office, where the registrar will ask your baby's name and place of birth and, if you are married, her father's occupation. If you are not married, both parents will have to be present to register. An interim birth certificate will be issued at the time, but you can obtain a full one for a small fee later on. It is best to register your baby as soon as you can, because after registration you can claim child benefit (£15 a week for your first child and £10 a week for subsequent children). The registrar will also give you a National Health Service number, which you should take to your GP practice in order to register your baby there too.

making a will

Apparently 70 per cent of us die without making a will. Dying intestate can cause problems for both your partner and your child regarding property, your pension and the guardianship of your child. It is vital, now you are becoming a parent, to make a will. Unless there are complications regarding your finances or your family, for instance adopted or step-children, then you can obtain a will document from the Post Office or from some stationers.

It is also important to appoint a guardian for your child in the event of both you and your partner dying, and their name should be detailed in the will. They should be someone your child is close to, who is young enough to cope with a small child and who has the same attitude to child-rearing as you do. Discuss possible candidates with your partner.

when to take maternity leave

Under the new laws, maternity leave has been extended to a more acceptable length with increased eligibility for additional leave, but the time still goes very quickly when you are getting used to parenthood, especially the first time.

The more time that you take off while you are pregnant, then obviously the less time you will have with your baby before returning to work. For this reason, many women remain at their jobs until the last possible moment before their baby is due. Whether this is sensible or not depends largely on the sort of work you do and how well you are during your pregnancy.

It is up to you when you start your maternity leave. The earliest that you can by law is 11 weeks before the birth but you can choose to work right up until the birth (subject to pregnancy-related sickness in the last six weeks). Remember, you may be entitled to parental leave and, if so, can tag this on the end of your maternity leave. Don't forget to give notice if you decide that you wish to take parental leave. Discuss this with your employer, and any decision that you make regarding this leave should be put in writing straight away.

physical stress

If you are employed in tiring physical work such as restaurant work, retail work or teaching, you could be putting your baby at risk of low birth weight or premature delivery, especially in the last three months of your pregnancy. Any job that imposes maternal fatigue will reduce the supply of oxygen and nutrients through the placenta to your baby. Always make sure, therefore, that you are taking your proper rest breaks at work, during which time you should sit with your feet up for an hour in the morning as well as an hour in the afternoon.

mental stress

Some jobs are not physically demanding, but are still extremely stressful. This can mean that you run the risk of high anxiety levels and raised blood pressure. Babies are affected by the stress hormones produced when we are under persistent stress, and the result can be poor neurological development, low birth weight, small head size and premature delivery. So don't assume that because you are merely sitting at a desk all day your job is not potentially damaging to you and your baby in the later months of pregnancy. Be honest in assessing how your job makes you feel. Are you under pressure to produce results in a highly competitive environment, and are you expected to do overtime and therefore work very long hours? If so, it would be best to start your maternity leave early to keep you and your baby safe.

travel stress

Your job may be reasonably undemanding, but how long does it take you to get to work? Do you have to stand up in a crowded rush-hour train for long periods of time, wait at bus stops, walk for long distances or climb stairs at stations at both ends of the day? This commuting will become more and more uncomfortable in the last months of your pregnancy and is therefore best avoided. Try and find an alternative route to work throughout your pregnancy and consider starting your leave earlier.

how long to take off

Most mothers find the weeks of maternity leave fly by, and they suddenly have to get into gear organizing childcare and facing the prospect of going back to work. This can be quite difficult as there hasn't been much time in which to get used to being a parent. Your baby may also seem very small to leave. If you do not feel ready to go back to work, you can discuss extending your leave with your employer by taking annual leave or parental leave, but you should never just do this without the prior agreement of your employer.

As has been said before, it is impossible to know how you will feel physically after you have given birth for the first time. Some mothers get back to normal very quickly, while some take much longer. A lot depends on the support structure you have in place, and it is wise to get as much help as possible in those first months. There is no merit in coping on your own if you don't have to, as you will just get overtired and both you and your baby will end up tense and anxious. So take up those offers of help from your nearest and dearest, especially if you want to be in a fit state to return to work.

delaying your return

There are some good reasons for delaying your return to work, but you cannot extend your maternity leave. OML at 18 weeks and AML at 29 weeks offer a protected right to return but you cannot change either as your rights would then be affected. You can take holiday or parental leave after the end of your maternity leave or see if your employer will agree to unpaid leave, which would be discretionary, but you would no longer have the right to return to the same or a similar job. Some sensible reasons for delaying your return to work, however, include health problems with your baby (or she has difficulty feeding), if you are dedicated to full-time breastfeeding, if you have taken longer to get back to normal than you thought, if your job is very demanding or if you are not happy with your childcare choices. Be sensible about this as there is no point in rushing back when all your instincts are telling you not to. Discuss it with your partner and family, and remember that the date that you go back to work is not written in stone. If you are too ill to return you can take sick leave. If you want different hours on your return because of childcare or breastfeeding then you can negotiate with your employer (see flexible working, pages 144–45 and part-time work, pages 146–47).

time off for illness

What happens if you are ill during your pregnancy or while you are on maternity leave? It is unlawful for an employer to sack you for being ill with a pregnancy-related illness, on the grounds of sex discrimination and unfair dismissal. If you suffer a miscarriage and are off work because of this, you should be covered too.

Obviously your employer must have been told that you are pregnant for you to be dismissed for a reason connected with your pregnancy, but you are protected regardless of the length of time that you have worked there.

sick pay during pregnancy

If you are ill and therefore absent from work due to a pregnancy-related illness in the last six weeks of your pregnancy, your employer can start your maternity leave automatically, regardless of the date that you wanted to begin it. But if you are ill before the 34th week, you will be on normal sick leave, even it if is pregnancy related. However, your employer may ignore the odd day's illness and not insist on you starting your maternity leave before you want to unless you are absent for a substantial period and it doesn't seem like you will be able to return before having your baby. Any illness connected with pregnancy should also be regarded separately from ordinary illness when recording your overall sick leave from work.

illnesses related to pregnancy

How do you convince your employer that your illness is pregnancy related? This is not easy, because women can suffer from conditions during pregnancy that also afflict the rest of the population, but theirs are nonetheless pregnancy related. One example of this is high blood pressure. This is usually caused by stress, a poor diet high in salt and saturated fats, being overweight and other factors, but a pregnant woman is vulnerable to hypertension because of the presence of the baby and placenta. If you have trouble convincing your employer that your illness is directly to do with your pregnancy, then get your doctor to write a letter confirming it that you can then show to your employer.

illness affecting your smp

If you are ill and off work for a substantial period during your pregnancy and so receive Statutory Sick Pay (SSP), paid by your employer at the rate of £60.20 per week, your average earnings will be below the minimum of £67 that you need to earn in the eight weeks before week 26 of your pregnancy to qualify for SMP. Your SSP may be topped up by your employer, so your earnings may qualify you for SMP, but your level of pay may still be lower than normal level, meaning your level of SMP will also be lower as it is based on 90 per cent of your pay. If you cannot get SMP, then apply for Maternity Allowance.

illness during maternity leave

You cannot claim SSP or employer's sick pay while on Ordinary Maternity Leave, although in some cases you can claim Incapacity Benefit. During Additional Maternity Leave you will not be able to claim SSP if you have not earned enough to qualify. If you are ill during this period, you may, however, be able to claim Incapacity Benefit from the Benefits Agency. Contact them for more advice.

illness on return to work

If you are too ill to return to work at the end of your maternity leave, you are still protected by the laws of unfair dismissal and sex discrimination. Once OML or AML expires, you are considered to be officially back at work, even if you are unable to go because of illness, so you would revert to your employer's normal sick rules. If you do not qualify for SSP you can claim Incapacity Benefit by presenting a doctor's letter at your Benefits Agency.

You should inform your employer that you are ill in the normal way, and send in a doctor's letter or certificate if necessary. Your employer's sick rules will then apply to you in the normal way. If your illness is pregnancy related then it cannot count against your general sickness record at work, nor can your employer sack you for not returning without then facing the possibility of an unfair dismissal and sex discrimination claim being taken up by you at some point.

time off for dependents

The new law that came into force in December 1999 states that all workers are entitled to unpaid leave from work to deal with unexpected or sudden emergencies, such as looking after a dependant who is taken ill or injured. No notice is required, because it is unforeseen, and the period you take off must be reasonable enough to deal with the problem and make any longer term arrangements. You do not have to have worked for any specific length of time, nor does it matter how many hours you work, to qualify for this right. Inform your employer as soon as possible why you are absent and how long you expect to be away.

if you have a premature baby

If you have had a premature baby and need more time off before returning to work, then you have several options. You could ask your employer for compassionate leave, which she could award at her own discretion but has no statutory requirement to do so. (Your contract may offer this possibility too.) You could use your holiday entitlement to extend your leave, or take your parental leave. You may be able to get a sick note from your doctor if the stress of having a premature baby has adversely affected you, and so could take sick leave. Inform your employer as soon as you know what extra time you might need so that you can both make appropriate arrangements.

premature babies

A premature, or pre-term, baby is one born before 37 weeks and up to one in eight pregnancies are pre-term. Prematurity is one of the most common threats to a baby's life because his organs may be too immature to cope with life outside the womb and his body weight may be too low to regulate his temperature.

Most premature babies have a low birth weight, with some weighing as little as 1kg (2.2lb). However, babies born as early as 24 weeks have been known to survive, helped by medical technology and expertise, although many do, sadly, develop handicaps.

coping with prematurity

It is a terrible shock going into labour weeks before you thought it was possible, and then having to endure the uncertainty of whether your baby will be able to survive on his own. Although your baby might be technically healthy before he is delivered, he can develop physical and mental handicaps from the rigours of delivery and postnatal survival, caused by such things as poor oxygen supply to his brain and infections.

Most women imagine their unborn baby to be round, plump and cuddly, so the shock of seeing a premature baby, with his fragile, loose fitting skin, poor colour and jerky movements, can be intensely difficult. It can also be very upsetting to see him pinned inside an incubator with monitors, intravenous lines and feeding tubes everywhere, and this also makes it difficult to touch or hold him. All your preconceptions about how you wanted to care for your baby have to be put on hold. Many women feel their baby just doesn't belong to them when they are in these intensive medical conditions. Nowadays close contact between parents and premature babies is encouraged, even if it is just stroking

CAUSES OF PREMATURITY

Many women go into labour prematurely for no apparent reason, but certain conditions predispose to premature labour.

- Abnormalities in the womb, such as an incompetent cervix, where the cervix is weak, or the womb is an abnormal shape.
- Multiple births, when the woman is carrying two or more babies, particularly with identical twins who are sharing the same placenta.
- Gestational problems such as a faulty placenta or excessive amniotic fluid.
- Maternal illnesses, such as having a high fever, suffering a urinary tract infection or experiencing pre-eclamptic toxaemia.
- Ruptured membranes caused by a physical trauma such as a car accident or fall.
- Smoking, high alcohol intake or drug abuse.
- Infections of the cervix or vagina.

your baby through the portholes of the incubator, and there are often facilities for you to stay in the hospital.

other considerations

A premature baby will throw your plans for when to start your maternity leave out of the window. Your baby is not going to be in the same state of development as a healthy baby by the end of your leave, and may need special care for many months. Your OML will start from the date that your baby is born if you are still working when you go into labour. AML is also calculated from that day. If your baby is born before you have informed your employer that you are pregnant, write to him as soon as you can, with the date of your baby's birth and the due date. Send a copy of the MAT B1 form if you have it, and a certificate from the hospital confirming the birth in order to start your maternity leave and Statutory Maternity Pay. (Page 99 has details of what to do if you need extra time off.)

Luckily most premature babies are born after 32 weeks, and have a good chance of leading a normal life. But don't be pressured into returning to work until you are certain that your baby is thriving.

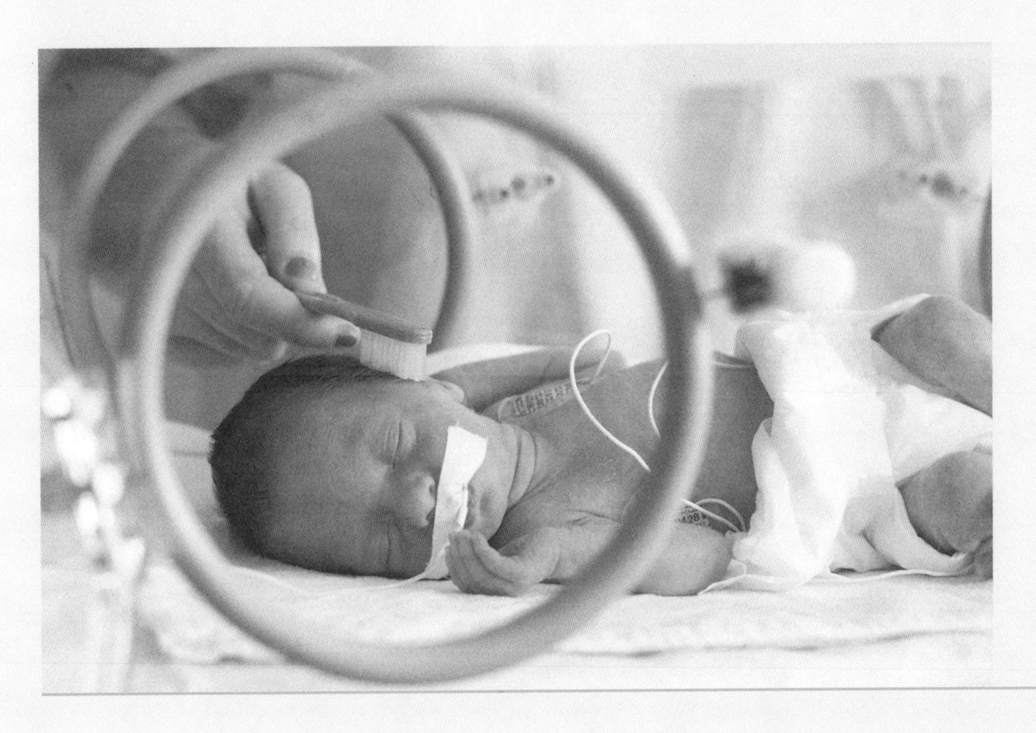

However daunting all those tubes look, you can still stroke and touch your baby in his incubator.

paternity leave

Paternity leave is leave taken by fathers at the time of their baby's birth. There is no legal right to paternity leave in either Britain or the United States yet but attitudes are changing as the importance of bonding with, and supporting, the family in the first crucial weeks is slowly being recognized.

However, fathers now have a legal right to parental leave (see page 91). Although it is usually unpaid, men can now take parental leave to be with their baby at the time of the birth. If your partner qualifies for this leave he can give notice to take it and his employer cannot postpone the leave for any reason. This new right reflects changing attitudes, and some employers now even offer paternity leave to their employees as part of their contractual benefits, although there is no legal obligation to do so. Your partner should check his company's policy. If your partner does not qualify for parental leave, he will have to use holiday time. This can be a problem if the baby is late or early, as holiday time usually needs to be booked in advance.

bonding

Although there are still some men who go green at the thought of being present at their baby's birth, many fathers have an active role in antenatal classes and labour, and also help

The closeness between your baby and her father is as special as the bond you have with them both.

take care of the baby afterwards. And some men, who believed they would be too squeamish and unable to cope with the process of birth, actually find that the extraordinary miracle of seeing their baby being born makes them forget their previous fears, and they are exhilarated by it.

If your partner is involved in every aspect of your pregnancy and labour, his chances of bonding with your child are greatly increased. Small babies are able to relate to more than one carer, and if your baby hears her father's voice throughout pregnancy, then has physical closeness and eye contact in the first weeks of life, she will soon form a firm bond with her father. Let your partner cuddle, feed and bathe the baby as much as possible early on, so that your baby begins to know him as well as you through touch, smell and sound.

support for you

Having your partner around during the first few weeks after the birth should mean you are freed from domestic tasks and can have proper time to rest, ignore the phone and the doorbell and have meals prepared when you need them. There is nothing more frustrating than finally putting a newborn down to sleep after the long process of feeding, changing and settling, only to find some well-meaning person on the doorstep dying for a chat and a cup of tea. Your partner can fend them off. Traditionally the woman's mother often comes to stay and fulfils these tasks, and there is nothing wrong with that if it suits everyone, but sometimes a new father can feel excluded from the process of fathering if there are too many women around and he is made to feel he does not have a role. If you both decide to have outside help, make sure that you also involve your partner in things.

parenting blueprint

The first few weeks after you bring your baby home is the time that a family blueprint for parenting is set up. The way in which you and your baby's father relate to each other as parents, and not just as lovers, begins as soon as the baby is born. It is tempting as a new mother for you to see caring for the baby as your territory. This is not from any conscious desire to exclude your partner, but, because you have been carrying the baby for nine months, given birth to her and may be breastfeeding, the bond can naturally be very close, especially if the father is not around much during that vital time. But if you start by making him feel redundant, that mothering is more important than fathering and his attempts to help with the baby are mocked if he makes a mistake, then this will be the blueprint that you will carry through your baby's childhood. Your partner will then probably choose to be less involved.

Conflict around parenting is very common, and often centres around the mother feeling that she has an unfair burden of labour, so start in the way you mean to continue, with a shared attitude toward being parents. And make sure that your partner feels that his input is just as vital as yours, because it is.

Taking your beautiful baby out of the rather impersonal hospital environment back to your own home is a very exciting moment. You will feel a proper family for the first time, and will be able to surround your baby with all the carefully chosen baby things that you have collected over the past months. You will also have the comfort of being able to sleep in your own bed and eat your own food.

However, it can also be a bit unnerving to suddenly be responsible for your baby without the medical team at the hospital to give you confidence if you are worried about something. So make sure that you have someone with experience of babies, such as your mother, a friend or your midwife, who you can call up and ask for help with those little worries that most mothers encounter at some time in the first few weeks. However silly your worries turn out to be, you will still value their reassurance. The most important thing is for you to be relaxed and confident, so that your baby can settle well.

Many parents are so thrilled with their little baby that they ask all their friends over in the first few days. It is, however, probably much wiser to wait until you have recovered from the birth a little and begun to establish a routine for your baby before allowing yourself to be inundated with visitors. You will be extremely tired when you first arrive home so make sure that you take it easy. Let others run round after you and don't worry about keeping up with all the domestic tasks.

First and foremost, enjoy the wonderful experience of being a mother and allow plenty of time for holding, kissing and cuddling your baby, as well as for feeding and changing. They are only small for such a short time after all.

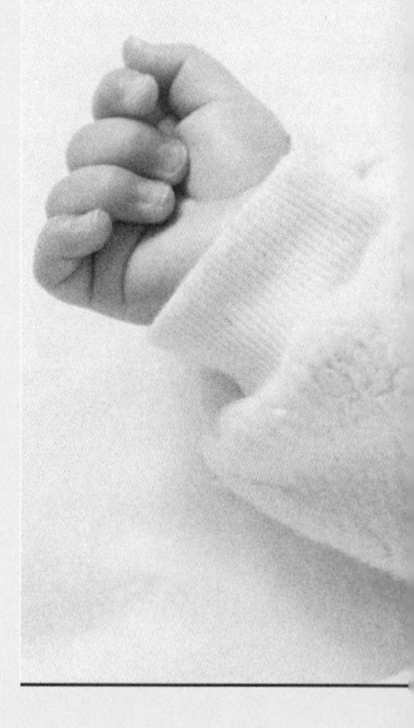

at home

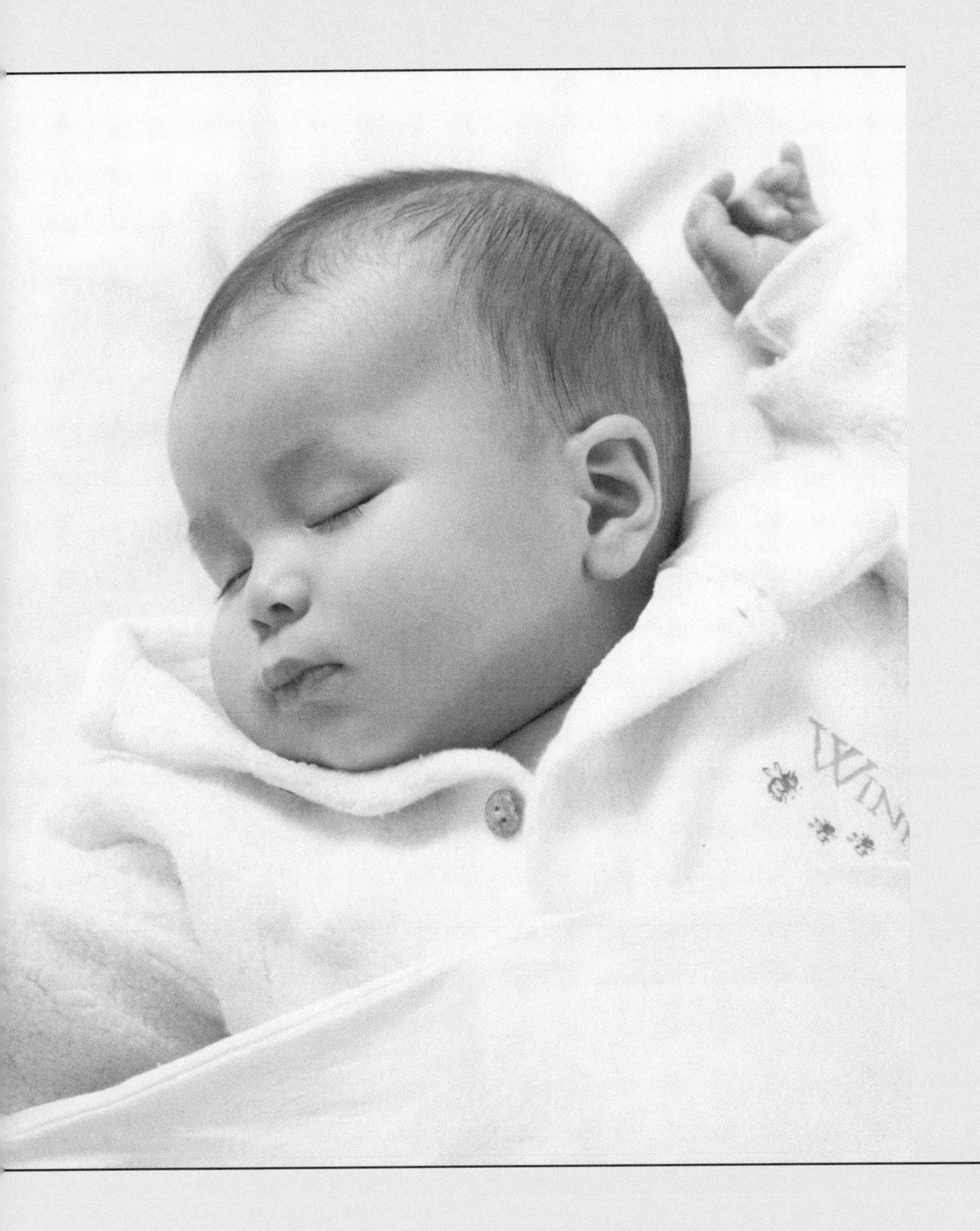

aftercare

Having a baby is extremely exciting and every new experience is memorable. However, you should be prepared for the fact that a new baby is very tiring. You will not necessarily be able to do everything that you want to do but if you just take your time and rest you will soon get into a routine.

If you have had a long, drawn out or difficult labour, or have worked up until the last minute before the birth, your energy reserves will be extremely depleted. Therefore you should accept all the help that you can get when you first get home, so that you can really enjoy this very special time.

rest

Many women think, before they give birth, that their baby will just slot into their lives, and that they will continue pretty much as they used to. However, having a baby will turn your world completely upside down. For the first weeks you will need to ensure that you get a lot of rest. No matter what time of day it is, when your baby sleeps, you can rest too. It is not the time to do the hoovering or to dig the garden. Sit quietly with your feet up, have a long bath or go to bed and sleep. It will take you longer to get your strength back if you don't take proper rest periods seriously at this very important stage.

your own health

As well as getting plenty of rest, it is also essential that you treat yourself with care by concentrating on getting your body back into shape and eating well. This is particularly important if you are breastfeeding.

Many women worry that they will never get their figure back after pregnancy, but this is not the time to diet, however horrified you are by your jelly-bag of a stomach. Your body naturally drops most of the extra pregnancy weight very quickly after the birth, especially if you are breastfeeding, and the rest will follow once you begin to move about more and exercise. If you eat a healthy diet then it won't be too difficult to get back to your original shape.

Your postnatal check-up is booked for around six weeks after the birth. During it your doctor will internally examine you to check that your womb has gone back into position and that your episiotomy or tear, if you had one, has healed properly. He or she should also ask about your general physical and emotional health and will advise you about contraceptives if necessary (see pages 116–17 for further discussion on this subject.)

inexperience

You will have gone to antenatal classes, and may have spent some time with other babies, but taking on the entire responsibility for the health and welfare of your newborn baby is an experience that nothing really prepares you for. You will naturally worry if he sleeps, or if he doesn't. Is he too hot or too cold? You wonder if you are feeding him adequately. Is he putting on enough weight, or too much, and what is that rash on his chin? Even tiny worries can be blown up into serious disasters when you are on your own, particularly if you are tired.

In the weeks following the birth you will get regular visits from your midwife. There will be a local mother and baby clinic you can take your baby to for weighing and general check-ups too. You will probably also have access to family or friend experience and support. Don't be afraid to call upon any of these resources if you have worries about your baby's health, or of your own ability to cope.

taking your baby out

Taking your baby out may seem like a simple enough task. Don't you just pop him in the pram and off you go? But you may be one of the many women who find going out with their new baby very daunting. Firstly you have to time it so that he is fed, changed and settled. Then you have to worry about wrapping him up appropriately, without making him too hot or too cold. But the biggest concern seems to be adjusting from being a woman on your own to being a woman with a pram. You may feel that crossing a busy road or negotiating the narrow aisles of the local supermarket is just too difficult to manage. You may also worry about whether he will wake up and cry when you are in a public place or panic about getting him and the pram on and off a bus. And how do you carry the shopping at the same time as pushing the buggy? It is very common to feel like this so just take it slowly, begin with short journeys and take someone with you initially to help. Be reassured that very soon you will feel you are missing something if you go out without your baby.

routine

Babies like routine, as it makes them feel relaxed and secure. If your baby is relaxed, the chances are that you will be too, and vice versa. No matter how often you feed your baby, try to follow the same routine of nappy changing, winding and settling each time, so that your baby knows what to expect. Bathe him and take him out at the same time each day, and keep the light, temperature and noise levels in his room consistent.

recovery time

See this postnatal period as a time of adjustment and recovery. Being a new parent is a learning process and, while it is a beautiful experience that you will never forget, you can't expect to be good at it overnight. You and your partner need time to get to know your baby and to establish yourselves as a family. Therefore your social life, housework and an excessive workload should be put on hold for at least the first few weeks. This will give you the chance to experience being a family, and will also enable you to build up your confidence as a parent.

psychological concerns

Try to accept that getting used to parenting takes time. You will experience many different emotions, which are described below, so don't set yourself unrealistic expectations about what you can achieve in this period. Above all, remember to concentrate on building a close and loving relationship with your baby and recovering your own equilibrium, both mentally and physically.

A great deal is said and written about the bonding process between mother and baby, with accounts of instant and intense bonding occurring the moment a mother sets eyes on her baby. For some this is how it happens, but there are as many other reactions as there are women experiencing them. You might have had a difficult and painful labour and part of you resents the little bundle who was the cause of your distress. You might just be tired or feel disillusioned by motherhood after the initial euphoria wears off, especially if your expectations were unrealistic. Not all women make natural mothers. If this applies to you, try not to feel bad about it. It often takes a while to settle into parenthood and create a close bond with your baby. You have to get to know each other gradually as you begin to gain confidence in your ability to handle her and keep her safe. And she will not stay at this needy, dependent stage forever. Babies quickly establish themselves and become much more self-sufficient.

Perhaps you are someone who will always find the demands of mothering difficult and there is no shame in that. It doesn't mean that you love your baby any the less, and a fair proportion of women would agree that it isn't plain sailing. Get as much support as you can in the areas you find problematic, and make sure you tell people how you feel.

self-image after childbirth

When you are heavily pregnant you long for the moment when your body is your own again and you return to your previous shape. It comes as something of a shock to discover that in the days after your baby's birth your stomach still feels as if you are six months pregnant, but is floppy and flabby and resembles a bag of jelly. As your hormones return to their non-pregnant state, you may also find that your hair, which became so thick and lustrous in recent months, starts to thin. Your chances of having either the time or the inclination to look after your appearance are slim in the weeks after the birth, and you have to accept that you will not recover your body immediately.

This might be all very well when all you are doing is feeding and sleeping and feeding again, but when the prospect of returning to work looms, you may go into a panic about how you look. Many women feel unattractive at this stage of motherhood. Don't be too hard on yourself – if you look around at women with children who are a little older than your baby, you will see that most of them have returned to their normal shape. Start your postnatal exercises, have a haircut, eat a healthy, nourishing diet and you will soon feel better about your appearance. When you get back into the swing of work and juggling your busy lifestyle, you won't have time to worry!

emotional roller coaster

Having a baby affects you both emotionally and physically. You will probably find your emotions are all over the place in the first weeks of motherhood; the smallest thing sends you off into either laughter or tears, and the intensity of the ups and downs can make you feel quite unstable. For instance, there is hardly a mother alive who hasn't sat up in the early hours of the morning with a baby who refuses to settle and had a sudden, desperate urge to throw her out of the window. Luckily the vast majority of us do not actually do it, but the feeling can seem very frightening at the time. You might worry that you will never be able to cope with work as well, but don't panic, your emotions will settle down quite quickly, and certainly in time for your planned return to work.

postnatal depression

For some women, at least one in ten, the emotional roller coaster described above doesn't naturally go away; instead it turns into something more serious and long term, which needs treatment. The problem is identifying the difference between normal baby blues and depression. If you feel hopeless and useless as a mother, look after your baby mechanically but with no enthusiasm, feel lethargic, have no appetite, are exhausted but can't sleep, find you get no comfort from others, cry a lot and have feelings of despair over a period lasting more than two weeks, then you must seek help as you are probably suffering from postnatal depression. Depression of any sort is an illness, so don't feel guilty. Counselling, anti-depressants and drugs to help you sleep can all be used effectively in treatment, so your first port of call is your doctor. And don't be afraid to tell those around you how you feel. You would tell them if you had flu.

time alone with your baby

When you go back to full-time work, you might find it quite difficult to have time alone with your baby. Once you get home your carer may have settled her for the night, and the mornings may be a frantic rush. But it is very important that you continue the bonding you began in those first months. Make some time by getting up a little earlier and taking her into bed with you for a cuddle. Ask your carer to schedule evenings in which you are able to bath and feed your baby when you get home and make sure your weekends aren't full of domestic tasks and socializing, so that you can enjoy quiet times as a family.

avoiding loneliness

For most women, having a new baby means being with him, thinking of him or talking about him for most of the day. You might ask, therefore, how anyone could get lonely with such a time-consuming companion. But babies, although very captivating to their nearest and dearest, are self-absorbed little beings.

Your baby has no interest in your state of mind, unless it has a negative impact on his nurturing, and he can't hold a conversation beyond the loving communication of gurgles and smiles. This is to be expected, but if you have been surrounded by people at work and home then suddenly having no one around but a tiny baby for perhaps 10 hours a day, five days a week, can make you feel isolated.

moving to a new area

This feeling of being alone can often be exacerbated by the fact that many women and their partners move house for reasons of space just prior to giving birth to their first baby. You might, therefore, find yourself in a new neighbourhood where you know nobody. Many of your friends may be work colleagues anyway, whom you socialized with after work in the locality of your job. Now they are all busy during the day, and don't understand your present concerns anyway. They are polite but bewildered if you talk about breastfeeding or nappy rash.

It is easy to become too reliant on your partner if you have no other outlet for company during the day, which can then put a strain on your relationship.

lack of confidence

Having a new baby can also affect your self-confidence. Perhaps you defined yourself by your work before, but now that you are a mother it feels difficult to start new friendships when you think you may only have babies in common. And you may not feel at your best; tiredness, extra weight, little time to buy new clothes and a persistent patch of your baby's regurgitation on your shoulder is not the most confidence-boosting combination! All of these feelings, however, are common and getting together with a group of new mothers will immediately show you how true this is. But first you have to find a suitable group. The best place to start is at your doctor's surgery, local health or sports centre, library or church where there will be plenty of information about mother-and-baby groups, activities such as mother-and-baby swimming lessons or massage sessions, local church get-togethers for new mothers and baby-and-toddler clubs of all sorts where you might meet people with the same interests as you.

If you don't feel comfortable in groups, then join a gym that has a crèche, take a few hours out for an adult education class or to

learn a new skill, or spend some time in the local playground and strike up conversations with the other women. Once you have one contact, others will follow more easily.

Getting together with other mothers and their babies is an important part of your new life as a mother. You will be able to share experiences and learn from one another.

taking your baby with you

Babies are quite mobile – you may not think so when you sit surrounded by prams, bottles, slings and nappies, but these days you can take them pretty much anywhere. Get a capacious shoulder bag for emergency equipment, then go and visit your friend for a few hours, take in a gallery or meet your partner for lunch. Many women quake at the thought of taking their baby on public transport, with the hassle of the pushchair and the worry of germs, but you will get used to it quite quickly. If you are finding it a problem, see the advice on page 107.

take time off

Loneliness can be greatly alleviated if you have regular treats to look forward to. Try and arrange for someone to babysit at least twice a week, so you can enjoy something that has absolutely nothing to do with motherhood.

Don't rush back to work because you are lonely until you have given these options a chance. Women are good at helping each other and enjoy getting together as much as possible. This gives them and their children company, and also offers a forum where problems and worries can be shared.

support groups and organizations

Support groups and organizations have come into their own these days, and there seems to be one for practically every problem. There are many well-established organizations that help with all aspects of being a mother, and they can be a very useful starting point if you are experiencing problems that your friends and family are baffled by or haven't the time to discuss.

The people that you will have contact with at these groups and organizations are almost always women who have been through the problem themselves. They will not only offer a sympathetic ear, but will also be able to put you in touch with others in your area who will understand and be helpful. In the case of organizations specifically aimed at children's illnesses or development problems, they will also be up-to-date with all the latest research and treatment.

Make sure you are familiar with the different groups available, so that you and your friends can take advantage of what they have to offer should the need arise. (All the addresses for the groups listed here can be found on page 157.)

your rights

Knowing your rights during pregnancy and as a new mother is vital, especially if you are planning to work through both. Although most employers are not out to cheat you of your rights, many simply haven't made themselves familiar with the current laws, which are changing in this arena more quickly than in most. The basics have been described in the section 'maternity legislation' on pages 86–103, but you may feel that you would like to talk things through further with an expert. The organizations listed below will be able to help you.

The Maternity Alliance is an excellent organization that aims to provide up-to-date information on all rights and benefits for the pregnant woman and new parents.

New Ways to Work is another organization that was formed to help women who want to combine motherhood with their career. It also commissions surveys of the current state of employment and flexible working for working mothers in Britain.

The *Health and Safety Executive* is a government-funded organization that provides detailed information about health and safety issues at work, including the laws regulating the workplace. There are hundreds of booklets that have been published by them on the subject of women at work. These informative booklets can be ordered from government bookshops such as Stationery Office Publishing.

support for the parents

There is another whole group of organizations that deal with supporting the family once the child is born. These could be helpful to you if you are under stress, are a single mother or do not feel supported by those nearest to you. Some of them run helplines where you remain anonymous unless you choose otherwise.

National Childbirth Trust (NCT), not only deals with pregnancy and labour but with many aspects of new parenthood too, including parenting education in schools.

Parentline supports any parent under stress and hopes to stop the situation getting to the point where the child is at risk of abuse and neglect by offering strategies for help within the family.

Gingerbread is a nationwide support organization for single parents that offers local self-help groups where you can meet those in the same situation as yourself.

Meet-a-Mum-Association (MAMA) also supports new mothers and those suffering from postnatal depression. It offers practical help with babysitting, lectures and also has social events where you can mix with other mothers like yourself.

La Leche League of Great Britain is an organization for mothers who want to breastfeed. There is a helpline and support groups plus personal, one-to-one help available. If you are thinking of breastfeeding, it would be a good idea to get in touch with them while you are pregnant for information and publications on the subject.

illness

If your child suffers from a disease or developmental condition, it is advisable to contact the specific organization that is concerned with that condition for any update on research and treatment options. You will also glean great comfort from talking to other mothers whose children are similarly afflicted.

The *Down's Syndrome Association*, the *Cancer and Leukaemia in Childhood Trust* and the *Foundation for the Study of Infant Deaths/Cot Deaths Research and Support* are a few such important organizations.

maternal problems

If you are suffering from mental or physical problems associated with pregnancy and childbirth, these organizations can help: the *Miscarriage Association*, the *Association for Postnatal Illness* and the *Toxoplasmosis Trust*.

legal advice

The following organizations can help you obtain legal advice on the problems that face pregnant working women: *The Citizens Advice Bureau*, *Equal Opportunities Commission* and *Law Centres Federation*.

Your local library will have lists of all of these organizations, and many more, and you should not be afraid of contacting any of them. They were set up originally because some particular need was not being addressed anywhere else, and they are mostly run by sympathetic people who have time to listen to you and can offer you relevant advice and support.

the importance of sleep

If you left work six weeks before your baby's birth and are going back to your job at the end of your Ordinary Maternity Leave of 18 weeks, you could be returning when your baby is only around three months old. There are babies in this world who reliably sleep through the night by this age, but unfortunately they are not, by any means, in the majority. So how do you get the sleep you need?

Not only will you probably be going back to work while your baby is so little she isn't sleeping through the night, but you may find you are still getting up on a regular, nightly basis when your baby has grown into a toddler. The effect of months or years of broken nights on an adult cannot be underestimated, especially when you have no opportunity for catching up on sleep during the day because you are in full-time work. You cannot predict whether your baby will be a good sleeper or a sporadic one, but you can certainly put in place some strategies early on that might minimize the habit of wakefulness and allow you to get a proper night's sleep.

sleeping in the family bed

By the late 1960s, childcare gurus like Dr Spock, with his rigid rules about feeding and sleeping that advocated a well-defined separation between mother and baby, were losing ground. And much of the more liberal debate on babycare centred round whether a baby should sleep in the family bed or not. Twenty years later the debate rages on, without any proof that having your baby in your bed has any definable safety advantage, or any disadvantages either. However it is certainly true that sleeping with your baby if you are drunk or using drugs to the extent that you are not aware of your baby's presence is potentially dangerous.

You will not stop your baby from waking in the night by having her in your bed, but she might wake you less because she is secure in your physical presence. And night feeds in which the baby is not moved from the sleepy, warm environment of the bed do not wake you or your baby so completely. However, if you start with your baby in bed with you, which is very tempting in those first few days, you will not find it easy to persuade her to

PUTTING YOUR BABY TO BED

Remember to put your baby to sleep on her back, as evidence suggests babies who sleep on their fronts are more at risk from Sudden Infant Death Syndrome (SIDS) and Sudden Unexpected Deaths in Infancy (SUDI) – see the glossary on pages 156–57 for a full definition of these. On no account allow anyone to smoke in or near your baby's bedroom as this is also a factor in SIDS.

ENCOURAGING NIGHT SLEEP

We all develop a body clock, known as our circadian rhythm, which means we sleep, for the most part, during the hours of darkness and are awake during the day. Babies develop this ability at different speeds, initially sleeping when and if they want to, regardless of day or night. Some parents go along with this and allow their baby to take her time, but you can encourage the process towards a normal body clock by making a distinction between daytime and nighttime in the way that you treat her, without imposing a rigid regime. Here are some pointers of how to do this.

- Make bathtime in the evening, and give her a leisurely and relaxing time to soothe her at the end of the day.
- Give her the evening feed in her bedroom, in the quiet, with the light down low and the temperature regulated so that it provides a cosy atmosphere.
- Put her to sleep in her pram during the day, and in her cot at night if possible.
- Don't make the evening or nights a time for boisterous talk and play as this might over-stimulate your baby.
- Make sure you burp her thoroughly after the last feed, so that you do not risk the added disruption of wind.
- Wrap her up properly in her cot, so that she feels secure without you.
- Do not leave her to cry for long periods if she does wake, especially when small, as this can lead to a wound-up baby who will take forever to settle.
- Have everything to hand at night, so the process of feeding, changing and settling is as short and efficient as possible.

sleep happily in her cot at a later stage. You might also find that such close proximity disturbs the quality of your own sleep as you are constantly aware of her presence.

You will just have to decide what suits you best. Alternatives include having the baby in a cot next to your bed, or letting her sleep in her own room with a baby alarm tuned in so that you can hear her cry. Whatever you do, avoid having her sometimes in one bed, sometimes in another, as this will just confuse her and compound the problem.

your own sleep

When you decide what you think is best for your baby, take your own sleeping patterns into consideration too before making your final decision. If you are a light or restless sleeper it might be better to separate yourself a little from your baby. Or, if you are worried you might roll over and injure her, then go for the cot option, because you won't sleep well if you are worrying. And make sure you get your partner to share in the night duties, particularly when you are back at work.

trust yourself

Be confident in your chosen treatment of your baby and she will respond well. Don't be tempted to behave in a certain way just because you think you ought to. Find out the pros and cons of each alternative, then follow your instincts. There are many different ways to raise a child successfully so don't feel pressurized into doing something that you don't feel 100 per cent happy with.

contraception after birth

Probably the last thing on your mind in the days and even weeks after you have given birth will be sex. This is actually a good thing as your body needs time to recover from what has been an unprecedented upheaval. However, you will eventually think about resuming sex and may be wondering how long you should wait and how breastfeeding and, perhaps, an episiotomy will affect your sex life.

When you first arrive home with your baby, your hormones will still be all over the place, you will be physically exhausted and psychologically your body will still belong, to some degree, to your baby. Therefore it is most likely that you will not want to resume sex straight away. Most men understand this and will be sympathetic, but if your partner feels somewhat displaced by your newborn baby he might be in a rush to have you back the way you were. Explain how you feel to him and make sure that you take the time to recover at your own speed. It is so important that neither you nor your partner worry about the lack of interest in sex right now, as your body will definitely return to normal given time.

You might, on the other hand, be keen to have sex. If this is the case then there is no medical reason why you should not resume sexual relations, including penetrative sex, as soon after the birth as you choose. There used to be a six-week advisory ban on penetrative sex, which was based on worries about infection and trauma, but it is now felt that this was overcautious advice. Whatever you decide to do yourself, however, you must think carefully about contraception before having sex again.

ovulation

It is a popular and highly dangerous myth that women are not fertile in the period after they have given birth, especially if they are breastfeeding. The fact is that you can begin to ovulate at any time and, because you ovulate two weeks before you have a period, thinking that you are safe until you have had your first postnatal period could lead to an unwanted pregnancy at a time when you are the least equipped to deal with it.

breastfeeding & contraception

If you are breastfeeding, you might not have a period until you stop feeding or reduce the number of times you feed. But, although your fertility will be reduced during this time, you still run the risk of pregnancy if you do not take precautions. Because the oestrogen in the Pill will affect your milk supply by reducing its production, you will not be prescribed the combined contraceptive pill during the time that you are breastfeeding. And although the progestogen-only pill obviously does not affect your milk in the same way, the effect these hormones might have on your baby are not yet known. Therefore it is perhaps better to stick to mechanical forms of contraception, such as a condom with spermicide or an Intrauterine device or diaphragm, which you can have fitted at your postnatal check-up six weeks after your baby's birth.

Fully breastfeeding your baby can be an all-consuming occupation, especially when you are adjusting to the process, and you may feel that your body is not really your own while you are supporting another life in this way. Breastfeeding mothers often express the feeling of being pulled in two ways if their partners do not understand this commitment and are anxious to resume sex too soon. Be open with your partner so that he fully understands if you feel this way.

feeling uncomfortable

If you have had an episiotomy, with or without a forceps delivery, you will almost certainly find penetrative intercourse uncomfortable or even painful at first. The stitches will take up to two weeks to dissolve, but occasionally they become embedded in the surrounding tissue. If you can still feel something spiky or sore after two weeks, or you subsequently experience pain during intercourse, you should see your doctor or midwife.

You may have an understandable fear of intercourse after an episiotomy, and the tension that you carry into the bedroom can cause real problems if your partner takes your reluctance personally. Tell him your fears and ask him to be patient. Have sex that does not involve penetration until you feel properly healed and confident, but, if the pain persists, do seek help from your doctor or midwife.

taking the lead

It is important that your partner follows your lead regarding resuming sexual relations after the birth. There are no rules as to when you will feel like sex again, and most variations are normal, so explain this to your partner and take the time you need; it is your body that has gone through big changes during this time. And always remember to protect yourself against an unwanted pregnancy.

THE MALE PILL

Scientists at Edinburgh University, who have been working on a male contraceptive pill, recently claimed that successful international trials held in Scotland, China, South Africa and Nigeria mean this pill could be available in Britain within the next five years. This pill is said to be 100 per cent effective and does not have any noticeable side effects. It contains a steroid, desogestrel, which inhibits sperm production, as well as testosterone, the male sex hormone, to maintain a normal sex drive. A male form of contraception such as this could be particularly useful for the partners of breastfeeding mothers, as the breast milk would then not be contaminated with hormones from the female pill.

breastfeeding

Whether or not you decide to breastfeed should not be dictated by your plan to return to work. You might think that because you will be going back to work it is better to get your baby used to the bottle and to other people feeding him right from the start. This is not true. Any period of breastfeeding, even if it is only for a few weeks, is better than none at all for both you and your baby.

Breastfeeding is the most natural and cosy way for your baby to bond with you, and you with him, so emotionally it is very comforting for both of you. But it is also excellent nutritionally for your baby. Even in the first few days after birth, before your milk comes in, your breasts produce a substance called colostrum, which contains all the protein, vitamins, minerals, water and sugar your baby needs. It also protects against bacterial infection and provides antibodies to all the diseases to which you are resistant, boosting your baby's immune system for the vital first months of his life.

Breast milk will also give him a head start if he is genetically predisposed to allergies, because your milk is specifically designed for him and protects his immature digestive system from having to deal with foreign bodies found in any other sort of milk.

When your baby sucks at your breast, your brain is stimulated to produce a hormone called oxytocin that makes your uterus contract, helping it to return to normal more quickly. Breastfeeding also encourages the extra fat laid down during pregnancy to be burned off, so you get your figure back faster.

possible fears

These days women hold down responsible jobs, have their own financial freedom and share the domestic burden with their partners. If you have been used to this then the absolute dependence your baby has on you when you are breastfeeding can seem quite demanding. Your body does not feel your own because you have to adapt your diet and keep up your fluid intake, take proper rest and regulate your life, both day and night, around your baby's needs. Breastfeeding is a serious commitment, certainly for the first three months when your baby is very small. But it still only amounts to a tiny proportion of your life, and gives a massive benefit to your baby's life. Women who have breastfed successfully, even for a short time, generally found the process to be unique and very special. And it just isn't true that you cannot go out or socialize when you are breastfeeding. Apart from theatres, cinemas and some restaurants, you can take your baby with you to most places these days.

You can also try offering your baby a bottle of breast milk instead of breastfeeding on a regular basis from early on, and he will then get used to taking a feed from a bottle. This will make it easier for your partner to take on some of the feedings, which will aid bonding.

convenience

Breastfeeding is also the most convenient way to feed your baby. It is so much easier than making up formula, sterilizing the equipment, worrying about the quantity, heating and cooling the bottle and storing it safely. Breast milk is there on tap, with the temperature, quantity and constituents your baby needs.

However, many women are fooled into thinking that because breastfeeding is 'natural' it must also be easy. For some it is, but for others it takes a lot of time and encouragement to feel confident. If you are having problems with breastfeeding, arrange to see a breastfeeding counsellor (your midwife will tell you who to contact) or talk to the La Leche League (see page 113).

work and breastfeeding

Full-time work and full-time breastfeeding are not usually compatible. Although you are protected by the same health and safety rights during breastfeeding that you were while you were pregnant, it is just not practical to have a small baby by your side when you are trying to do a full-time job, or even some part-time ones, unless you are lucky enough to have an on-site crèche at your workplace.

However, there are solutions if you are keen to continue the process after your maternity leave ends. You can cut down your baby's feeds and only breastfeed in the morning and the evening, replacing the feeds in between with formula. Or you can express milk for the feeds that you will be absent for by employing a breast pump and storing the milk in sterilized bottles in the fridge for up to two days. Breast milk also freezes well.

There is no reason why you shouldn't successfully combine bottle and breast once your milk supply is properly established. One word of warning though, breastfeeding depends on the principle of supply and demand, so if you replace feeds with formula too regularly, or before breastfeeding is properly established, your milk supply will diminish and you will find yourself having to top up with formula more. This can easily be remedied, though, by putting your baby to the breast more often until the supply recovers.

Some women struggle with the whole idea of breastfeeding and would rather not try at all. Others do try but they have terrible trouble with cracked nipples and mastitis (breast infection) and become disheartened and depressed by the process. If you decide to bottlefeed, whatever your reason, please don't feel guilty about doing so. Breast milk might be best, but not at any price. Formula baby milk has been refined and adapted to be as much like breast milk as possible, and most babies thrive on it. But if you can manage to breastfeed, even for the first four weeks, you will have given your baby the best start that you possibly can.

nappies

If you are thinking of returning to work, it is important, when deciding which type of nappy to use, that you take into account your carer's time and facilities as well as your own. There is no proof that one type of nappy has the advantage over another, as long as the nappies that are used are changed regularly and the baby's skin is properly cleaned and dried each time.

disposable versus reusable

For a while disposable nappies were all the rage and everyone wondered how they had coped with all the mess and labour of washing fabric ones. But then concern over environmental protection was raised and many people, worried at how the mountain of plastic was to be disposed of, went back to cloth nappies. It also became apparent that disposable nappies were more expensive in the long run than fabric ones, although the initial outlay on cloth nappies is higher.

However, this is not a simple black and white issue. The environmental question of disposal must be weighed against the energy expended on washing, rinsing and drying fabric nappies, not to mention the vast quantity of washing powder, bleach and sterilization materials flushed into the drainage system. Cloth nappies also require plastic pants as waterproof protection.

From the financial point of view you also have to take into account the ongoing cost of washing and drying the cloth nappies. The overall cost is not just what you paid for them, but also the energy that is used to clean them. However, you can use the same nappies for any subsequent children.

disposable nappies

These nappies are easy to use as they have elasticated legs and sticky tabs or Velcro for fastening. Be careful how you dispose of them, as they do not flush down the toilet. There are now deodorized plastic bags available for this purpose, especially useful if you are leaving your baby with someone else.

If you are planning childminder, crèche or nursery care for your baby, it is advisable to choose disposable nappies, at least during the periods you are at work. If you have a live-in nanny or au pair you can probably call the shots about whether disposable or re-usable nappies are used, but remember that the process of washing and drying nappies is very time-consuming and you might prefer your carer to do something else about the house.

cloth nappies

Cloth nappies come in various different types. There are the plain terry-towelling squares, which usually require a muslin square or disposable paper liner for comfort and have to be folded and fastened with a pin. The shaped terry nappies have a reinforced central panel for absorbency, and are fastened either by pin or popper. These are easier to put on as you don't have to fold them into shape. And there are also all-in-one ready-shaped cloth nappies that are backed with plastic and fastened with poppers or Velcro, but are still washable.

You will need to soak soiled nappies in a bucket full of diluted sterilizing solution before putting them through the hot-wash cycle on your washing machine. Muslin squares, even if you are using disposable nappies, are a useful 'mopping up' item.

Nappy services are an option if you wish to use fabric nappies. Unless you live in a very isolated area, the service will pick up your soiled nappies every day and drop off clean ones. The cost is comparable to top-of-the-range disposable nappies.

folding a cloth nappy

Fitting a bulky terry cloth nappy to a very small baby's bottom can seem quite difficult, and in the first week or so, depending on the size of your baby, a muslin square with a paper liner will probably provide sufficient absorbency. As your baby grows and needs extra absorbency, you can begin to use the terry cloth squares, either with a muslin lining as well as a disposable paper one, or just a paper lining. The first few times you change your baby's nappy you will be all fingers and thumbs, because babies do not lie still and often hate being unwrapped and fiddled with. But soon it will be second nature. Make sure your partner has plenty of practise too. Paper nappy linings are a useful way to flush away your baby's soiling and reduces the staining on the cloth nappy. There are two ways to fold a nappy; either in a simple triangle shape or in a kite shape, which often fits babies better. If you are using a muslin square as well, fold it identically to the terry cloth square and lay it on top of the terry cloth, or just fold it in a rectangle and use it like a liner.

triangle shape Fold a corner of the terry cloth or muslin square over until it is in line with the opposite corner of the square, forming a triangle.Then lie your baby on the nappy and bring up the lower end between her legs, fold in the two long points on either side, and fasten the whole nappy with a pin in the centre. At first you will have to tuck in the extra nappy ends until your baby grows to fit the nappy better. When she gets bigger, a pin on each side might be necessary.

kite shape The kite shape makes a neater, less bulky shape to fit to your baby. Lie the terry or muslin square flat with the corners pointing north, south, east and west. Take the east and west points and fold them inward to form one long point, like the bottom of a kite. Then fold over the remaining point at the top. Lie your baby on the nappy, and bring the long end between her legs, folding the pointed tip inward if it is too long. Then bring the other two corners across the front and fasten all three with a pin.

a network of support

No one knows you like your own mum and her support will be invaluable to you in the weeks after your baby is born, as is that of the rest of your family. You may also have decided that you are not going to be the main carer of your child. If your partner, or outside help, will look after your baby when you go back to work, then how will your different roles fit together?

support in the first weeks

Your own mother will understand better than anyone when you are feeling low and, ideally, can provide domestic support as well as confidence and wisdom when you are in the immediate recovery stage following your baby's delivery. Talk it through with her before the birth, and work out how you both think she could be most useful. For instance, she could cook some meals and put them in the freezer, answer the phone and deal with visitors to the house and supervise the washing and drying of the mountains of baby clothes and sheets. However, you should remember that you can't fire your mother! Be careful not to get carried away by the sentiments of giving birth and ask your mother to stay for a protracted period, especially if you are not, and never have been, particularly close, or if your mother and your partner do not have a good relationship. Ask the advice of your partner and siblings before committing to any arrangement.

Don't ignore the potential support of relatives aside from your mother, such as sisters, aunts and parents-in-law either. It is easy to leave the in-laws out in the cold when you are dealing with postnatal adjustment, especially if you do not have a particularly cosy relationship with them. But they are just as much grandparents to your baby as your own parents are, and if you leave them out you can cause a lot of unnecessary distress.

You are allowed to be a bit demanding in this period, and marshal as much loving support as you can get. Without letting your relatives dominate you and tire you out, let them in on your new baby, so that they too can form the close and important bond that the extended family can have with your child.

The flip side of the coin, however, is when a relative tries to bully you into treating your baby in a way your instinct knows is wrong. Telling you you must only feed your baby four-hourly instead of on demand is a great favourite. Perhaps this worked for your relative, but that doesn't mean you have to bring your child up the same way. Listen to advice, but then do what you feel is best.

longterm childcare

Mothers are still the usual carers of children, but most research suggests children are happy with many different arrangements, so long as the care is consistent and the child feels loved and respected. Because men do not get pregnant, they often feel excluded from the female mystique of pregnancy and childbirth right from the moment of conception. By the time the baby is delivered, the bond the mother has with her baby can be a million times more developed than the bond the father has. The mother/baby relationship can then be enhanced by breastfeeding, but the man can be in danger of feeling superfluous.

Before your baby is born, sit down and explain how much you want your partner to play an active part in parenting. Tell him that you are whistling in the dark as much as he is, and that you will need to support each other. Your partner might feel all fingers and thumbs with a tiny baby at first, but if you give him a chance he will be just as adept at nappies and feeds as you are. If you are breastfeeding, express your milk sometimes so that your partner can also experience the delights of feeding his baby.

father as main carer

If you are earning a much higher income than your partner is and have good career prospects, if he can work from home or he isn't happy in his present job, it is certainly worth considering him being the main carer. You will both have to take into account how you will cope with the jokes and jibes about men doing 'women's work', and understand that much of the support network for childcarers is directed entirely at women. How will he fit in at the mother-and-toddler group for example? If he doesn't, he risks being isolated and lonely. Then again, times are changing, albeit slowly.

other influences

With the disappearance of the tight-knit, supportive, family community, friends are taking over many of the childcare roles and relationships that previously relatives saw as their domain. Often families live many miles away, and their support is only sporadic or at a distance. But we all need people who are more experienced in child-rearing than we are, people to whom we can turn for advice and other adults who can form relationships with our children as they grow up. Friends whose children have left home or who do not have children are often a good source of support because they are not busy with their own families. Let them know how important their contribution to your family is, and include them in your children's milestones.

keeping in touch

Sometimes we forget how close a bond a child can make with someone who looks after him, or visits him regularly when he is small. As an adult, particularly a busy one, it is easy to forget the nanny-before-last, or the neighbour next door to your previous house who had your child to tea twice a week. But your child probably won't. Make sure he understands why he does not see them so much anymore and that he has had a chance to say goodbye properly. If possible, keep in touch with the occasional card or phone call.

an older sibling

It is probably true that your existing child, whatever her age, will not initially thank you for bringing home a new baby. However you rationalize it, and whatever terms you couch it in, the fact is that your older child now has to compete with her sibling for your love and attention. So what can you do to ease this process?

There is no use in pretending it is otherwise, but many parents fall into the trap of trying to persuade their older child that having a baby sibling is going to be enormous fun. Then, not only does the child feel the normal jealousy at being supplanted, she also feels cheated out of a supposed treat. However, you do not have to depress your child by anticipating their jealousy with adult explanations of doom and gloom, as this experience is beyond her understanding and you will only confuse her. What you can do is make her as secure and independent as possible, within the limits of her age, so that she is able to cope with the new arrival from a position of confidence. Here are some suggestions:

- Make sure you tell your child about the impending birth, and that she does not glean confusing tit-bits from your conversations. It is best, though, that you wait until you are six months pregnant to do this.

Involving your older child in many of the preparations for your new baby will make her a lot more enthusiastic about her little sibling and will also make her understand that she still has an important role in the family.

- Don't leave it until the last minute before settling her in her own room. You can make this a positive experience by involving her in the choice of colours and pictures. Try and get her settled way before your due date.
- Let her snuggle up to your growing tummy and feel the baby moving, discuss possible names with her and speculate about what the baby might look like.
- If you are going to employ a carer for the first time, make sure that they get to know each other well in advance of the birth. Being handed over to a stranger and losing her mum to a whingeing, attention-seeking bundle could be the last straw.
- Try and get your partner to take some time off around the birth so that he can spend lots of time with the older child.
- Above all, be honest about what a pest this baby will seem to his sibling for the first few months. Many parents try to get their children interested by telling them they will have someone to play with, but there's not a lot of playing to be done with a tiny baby. Having a close and loving relationship with your existing child will do much to allay her mistrust of the new baby, and very soon her joy in her sibling's company should override her initial fears.

guilt

Juggling your own postnatal emotions and that of your older child can be extremely hard. You feel desperately guilty that your child is clearly upset and feeling supplanted and rejected, but there is only so much you can do to assuage this at the same time as caring for your newborn and yourself.

Remember that it is perfectly reasonable of you to want another baby and to love him as you did your firstborn, and in the long run your child will be pleased she has a sibling. This is where your partner can be of immense help, as can other members of the family, such as grandparents. Not only can they care for the older child, but they can also take over the babycare for periods to allow you to have time alone with your oldest. This is always important, however old the child.

your child's school

If your eldest child is starting nursery school, make sure it does not coincide too closely with her sibling's birth. She will need lots of attention during this time. And please don't forget to allow time off from work to attend any school functions she might have, however young she is. There is nothing more likely to build unhappiness and resentment in a child than her parents' absence when other children's parents turn up.

getting used to each other

The difficulties of having more than one child, particularly if you are working, is that a lot more of your time will be required on the domestic front. However, the advantage of a second child is that you have the mechanism for parenting in place and will feel a lot more confident. Your children will quickly get used to one another and you will be building the family that both you and your partner want.

The moment has come when you have to decide whether to throw yourself back into your job and allow someone else to care for your baby, or to take some time off from your career to be a mother, either part-time or full-time. At this stage you will not know how it is going to feel either way. You have just experienced perhaps the biggest upheaval of your life by becoming a mother, and nothing will ever be the same again, so the ideas that were formed when you were still pregnant and working may no longer apply now.

You may be surprised to find yourself one of those mothers who can't wait to get back to work, or you might have thought you would be itching to return and find yourself dragging your heels at the thought of your office schedule. Most of us, however, feel ambivalent about the reality of going back at first. You will probably find your maternity leave has flown by and that you can't believe it is almost time to return to work. Your baby may also seem pitifully small to leave, even in the competent hands of your chosen carer. And leaving him will be a wrench at first. But don't worry, your feelings are perfectly normal.

Whatever you decided before you gave birth, please remember that you always have a choice. You may have to work for financial reasons, but the sort of work you do and the hours in which you do them can be tailored to suit your new life as a mother, not the other way round.

In this section we look at the factors, both emotional and practical, that a new mother should consider before making the decision to return to work. If you are fully aware of the hurdles that you might face, you will be better equipped to deal with them successfully.

returning to work

whether to return

Work will have been the last thing on your mind in the first weeks after your baby is born and you are getting used to a different role. But time will go unbelievably fast in this period, and soon the questions of when, how and, indeed, if, you will return to your old job loom in front of you.

Perhaps the decision to return or not seemed very straightforward before you left work, and the months off sounded perfectly adequate for getting your baby settled, but at that stage you were not dealing with all the facts. One crucial element was absent from the decision process, and that is how you feel about being a mother. The intensity of your attachment to your baby has probably taken you by surprise, and it is a unique feeling that you will have never experienced before. Only when you factor your feelings about motherhood into the equation will you be able to make a sensible decision about your return to work. A recent Gallup poll found that 20 per cent of women who planned to return to work changed their minds after their baby was born.

to work or not to work?

The debate about whether children suffer from having a working mother rumbles on. Numerous studies, most purely based on the educational achievement of the children studied, have had inconclusive results. Some say a child of a working mother does less well, but others have found the exact reverse. This lack of consensus is hardly surprising as so many different factors are involved in creating a happy and successful human being, not just the role of the mother. There are no studies, for example, that have examined how a father's working commitments can impact his children.

So the best thing seems to be to ignore research and follow your instincts about whether to work or not. If you feel very strongly that you should be with your children when they are small, then don't be swayed by the fact that so many mothers work these days. On the other hand, if you really long to go back, then do so with a clear conscience. There are some things to remember when you are deciding. For example, your baby won't benefit from your being unhappy. There are more ways to work than just full-time, away from the family home. And you can always change your mind if you find you don't like being away from your baby. But your baby will not always be so small; in a few years he will be at school most of the day and you will feel quite differently about leaving him.

advantages of working

Presuming you enjoy your job, working will bring you stimulation and satisfaction, and will also bring a degree of financial independency. By not taking extended time off from your work you will be ensuring a smoother path up the career ladder and will avoid having to break back into the job market at a later date. You will also continue to have financial independence. If you give up a job you love and find being a mother difficult, you will be miserable at home and your baby will not benefit from this.

get your partner's support

Even in this day and age, there are plenty of men who, for one reason or another, dislike the idea of their partner working instead of staying at home with the children. If you have decided that you want to return to work and your partner is like this, try to get to the bottom of why he feels this way. He might have had a bad experience with his own carer as a child or he might just be plain jealous of your other interest. Your task is going to be very much harder if your decision to work is constantly being undermined and you are getting no support from your partner as a result. You have as much right to work as he does. Tell him how much your job means to you, and how unhappy you will be if you do not go out to work.

advantages of staying at home

The stresses and strains of juggling both work and being a mother can be extremely draining. If you stay at home you are in control and can run to your own schedule instead of having the inconvenience of rigid working hours. You may also then have the chance of taking further education or training courses that might give you more work options in the future and have time for your own pursuits.

By choosing to stay at home you are there for your baby at all times and will get to know him very well, which will create a much more relaxed form of mothering. Many women who work full-time are quite nervous of their children because they have not built up the day-to-day familiarity that they would have as a full-time mother. You also avoid the time-consuming and stressful process of organizing good childcare by doing it yourself.

financial considerations

You may have no choice about whether you work or not if you are the sole provider for your baby but, even if you are not in this situation, there are always financial factors to consider. Many women think that they need to work to maintain their present lifestyle, even if they are unhappy working and being a mother. Look carefully at what you would be giving up financially if you left your job. You and your partner might find that the luxuries you thought you needed could be dispensed with for the time being. And does the amount you earn once childcare has been deducted make a significant difference to your financial stability anyway?

Everyone has their own version of what 'quality of life' means. There are no rules, but try to guard against following a path against your better instincts that you could live to regret. There are always other options.

what if you change your mind?

You are all geared up to go back to work at the end of your maternity leave, but as the date gets closer, you begin to have your doubts. The thought of leaving your baby to go back into the world of work suddenly seems very unappealing. What should you do if you feel like this?

Should you just bite the bullet and go anyway, against your better instincts, or should you cancel the childcare and stay at home? The first questions to ask yourself if you are beginning to dread the thought of returning to work are: Why am I working? Is it just for the money? And what is the reason for my reluctance to return?

It is important to work out your motivation for deciding either to stay at home or to return to work, as this will affect how successful you are in juggling your baby, your relationship and your job. Don't do either just because you think you ought to and then be miserable. Your baby will not appreciate having a martyr for a mother. But if you do decide to stay at home, what are your rights as far as your maternity pay is concerned?

paying back maternity pay

Whatever your decision about returning to work, your Statutory Maternity Pay is yours and there are no circumstances in which you will have to repay it. This includes the first six weeks at 90 per cent of your pay, and the last 12 weeks of £60.20. If you decide not to return, you will only have to pay back any additional maternity pay that your employer gave you on top of the SMP, but, even with this, you only have to return it if a pay-back condition was written into your contract before the event. So you can resign from your job in the normal way, and your notice period can run at the same time as your maternity leave, which means that you do not have to return to work.

loving being a mother

You may simply feel that you do not want to leave your baby at this stage. You may be loving motherhood so much that you know you would be miserable swapping it for the workplace. In which case you should follow your instincts and hand in your notice at work. You may feel differently in a year or so, but what is right for you and your baby now is the most important consideration. You don't want to look back on his quickly vanishing babyhood and regret that you didn't listen to yourself at this time.

is it the job?

Jobs can seem much more entertaining when there is no alternative occupation, but now that there is a beautiful and fascinating baby to care for at home, perhaps your job is shown up for what it was all along, boring. If this is the case, you would probably be better off resigning and waiting for a better time to look around for a different one.

Before you had your baby, your identity may have been very tied up with your job. And others do tend to categorize us by the sort of work we do. If you got used to a particular work identity, one of the reasons you were so keen to go back to work before you gave birth may have been a fear of losing that identity. But becoming a parent is often a very confidence-boosting process for both parents, and you may no longer feel that you need the external badge of work outside the home to feel good about yourself. So if your job was not particularly compelling in itself, you may be happier being a full-time mother for now.

poor conditions

It may be the long hours that you often had to work that are putting you off your job. They seemed fine when you had nothing else to do, but they are now impossible because of your childcare responsibilities. Your employer is bound by law, under the Sex Discrimination Act, 1975, to listen to your suggestions for a more flexible way of working, for instance part-time work or job-sharing. These are discussed in more detail on pages 144–49.

inadequate care provision

Perhaps you are secretly not happy with the carer you have chosen. You may have wanted a nanny at home, but can only afford a childminder, and this is worrying you. The nursery, which seemed such a pleasant and happy place when you were pregnant, now seems too noisy and threatening for your small baby. Talk to your partner about your worries, and, if you really want to work, try and find some alternative care for your baby. Perhaps there is a relative who could help out for a while until you are more confident about leaving her with a stranger.

There are some women who are genuinely concerned that their baby will become too attached to their carer while they are at work, and will therefore cease to love them. As a result they are very ambivalent about any closeness they perceive between their baby and carer. This possessiveness will only be detrimental to your baby, and is anyway unfounded as children always recognize their mother as their prime carer, even if the time you spend with them is less than the nanny does. If you feel so insecure, perhaps you should stay at home until you are more confident about the bond that you have with your child.

changing your mind

Don't forget that you can change your mind about working. What is important is that you are as happy as possible with your lifestyle because if you are happy and fulfilled, then your children will have the best possible environment in which to grow and develop. Follow your instincts and do what is right for you and your family.

easing back into work

As you prepare to go back to work, there are lots of things that you will need to organize, but take your time and try not to worry. You may realize once you get back to work that you don't want to leave your child, but there are alternatives, so don't panic if you do feel this way. Whatever your emotions as your date of return looms, follow the advice here so it is as stress-free a time as possible.

flexibility is key

If you decide that you are only planning to go back to work to avoid boredom, then perhaps you should consider a part-time job, or check out alternatives such as studying or learning another skill. If you decide it is the income you need, you have to weigh up the costs of childcare and the hidden costs that are involved, such as food and general facilities for the carer. If you are worried about damaging your career prospects, you must take into account the possible stress on yourself that balancing a full-time career and a family might mean.

Whatever you decide, be flexible. If, in a few months' time, you find you have made the wrong decision, then be prepared to be openminded about other options. Your children won't be young forever; their needs change quite quickly, and so can yours.

separation

However much you look forward to going back to work, separating from your baby for the first time will be very upsetting. It can feel as if there is an invisible cord pulling you straight back to your baby, and you might suffer dreadful pangs of sadness and guilt that you have abandoned your baby to another's care.

Being anxious at the beginning of this process is natural, but, if you are confident in your choice of carer, your baby will be safe and happy. As previously stated, babies can be loved and cherished very successfully by people other than their mother.

You will find that your anxiety lessens as you get used to your work routine. If it doesn't then you must ask yourself if you are happy with the carer you have chosen, or if you would actually prefer to be with your baby full-time yourself.

planning your day

One of the keys to successfully returning to work is thinking ahead. Time is your first consideration. If you don't have live-in help, make sure that you allow at least half an hour between your carer arriving and you leaving for work. Otherwise there is no proper time to hand over and tell the carer about how your baby is and what needs doing about the house during the day. Notes on the kitchen table are not a good substitute for this personal interaction. And it also means that if your carer is held up for any reason, you will not be panicking.

Remember to ask for all the help and support you need too as parenting is a joint venture. Your partner might be rushing out of the door to go to work, but that doesn't mean he shouldn't sometimes do the takeover with the carer and allow you to get to work early.

organizing yourself This is another difficult area. You will have to work out how long it takes you to get up, wash, dress and deal with your baby without rushing. Make sure you leave plenty of time for this. Gone are the days when you could hurl yourself out of bed, grab some toast and run for the bus. If you are tense with your baby because you are pressurized about time, she will sense it and play up, taking up even more of your time. This is especially true if you are still breastfeeding in the morning and evening. Your anxiety can also affect your milk supply if you are expressing milk for your baby during the day (see pages 118–19 and 139).

daily provisions Running out of milk or nappies will only add to your daily stress. Either organize your childcarer to do shopping for you each day, or work out a time when you and/or your partner do a weekly shop.

housework This is another consideration when you first return to work. Many people cannot afford separate cleaners, so try and find someone who will help out with some of the housework while they are looking after your baby, even if this means paying them a little bit extra. Alternatively, you could divide the chores between yourself and your partner. Don't put yourself in the position that so many women do of feeling that you must be superwoman, and run the house by yourself as well as doing a full-time job. Agreeing on a list together of how the house tasks and baby-related activities can be divided up can help avoid arguments and recriminations about whose turn it is.

tiredness

It is probably inevitable that you will feel very tired when you first return to work. Don't expect too much from yourself; it will be a while before your energy levels get back to normal as your body has just been through a vast upheaval. Avoid too many social events, take naps whenever you get the chance and take a relaxed attitude to the housework. It really doesn't matter if everything isn't perfect for a while. And make sure that you are eating a healthy nutritious diet within your tight schedule, as it is essential that your body gets adequate fuel for your busy lifestyle.

Remember that your baby's needs must always come first, but you must also look after yourself, plan carefully, share tasks, ask for help when you need it and avoid taking on anything extra. You are hopefully going back to your job because you want to, so enjoy it.

investigating childcare

Making the right choice about what form of childcare will best suit you, your partner and your baby is crucial to the success of your return to work. To make that decision, there are various factors to take into consideration – these are all discussed in detail below.

the overall cost

You will obviously have to calculate childcare costs against your earnings. There is no point in having a carer who is earning more than you do and thereby creating a financial deficit. But you also cannot compromise your child's happiness and safety by skimping on the quality of her care. Childcare costs are high in Britain, and women spend on average up to 50 per cent of their earnings in this arena. Costs vary, depending on where you live and how many hours you want the care for. A trained nanny is the most expensive option. Depending on whether they live in or not, expect to pay between £100–400 a week. At the other end of the scale is an untrained au pair, who will be paid up to £70 a week, while nurseries and childminders fall somewhere in between. Only grannies and aunts might possibly come free.

environment

You will also have to decide where you want your baby to be cared for. If you feel very strongly that you want them to be at home, then you will have to opt for the nanny or au pair option. If you decide on care away from home, make sure that the environment you are placing her in is satisfactory. Check it out carefully and ask yourself questions such as: Does anyone smoke there? Are any animals or other children in the home being properly supervised? Is it clean and free from hazards such as unprotected stairs or dangerous electrical equipment? Is it properly heated? A registered childminder will have had her premises thoroughly checked, but you should also do your own survey. The way someone lives tells you a lot about the sort of person that they are.

Nurseries are carefully regulated, but spend some time in a selection of them before you choose one. Try dropping in unexpectedly at least once, to assess the noise levels, the attitude to rowdiness and indiscipline in the other children and to see how much time is spent outside. It is also important to check the child/carer ratio and see how that ratio might be managed in relation to your own child.

travelling

It is important to decide where your childcare should be situated. Most couples opt for somewhere near their home, but it may be more sensible to find someone nearer either your or your partner's work. Make sure your carer's home or the nursery is easily accessible on public transport too.

temporary care

It will take your baby a while to get used to a new carer, and it is traumatic for a small child to lose someone they have grown fond of. There is also the stress for you of finding someone else to replace the carer if he or she leaves. Obviously you cannot expect prospective carers to guarantee a lasting commitment, but, wherever possible, choose carefully and avoid short-term care.

finding your carer

It can be a very difficult and stressful process to find the right person for the job, because good childcare is at a premium. You can go through a nanny or au pair agency, which will cost money but will weed out anyone with dodgy references or inadequate qualifications. (You should still check the references yourself, no matter what the agency says.) Or you can advertise in your local newspaper, newsagent or in publications such as *The Lady,* which advertise domestic help. This can trigger a deluge of phone calls, and it is very time-consuming and arbitrary picking suitable interview candidates. Alternatively, you can go through word-of-mouth, but again, be rigorous in reference-checking. If possible, have your partner, friend or a relative present when you interview to get a second opinion, and don't be shy about asking the person back for another interview just to make sure your original perceptions about them are still right.

sharing your home

If you decide to have residential childcare, which offers you more flexibility in how you come and go yourself (essential if your job has unpredictable hours or locations), you must take into account that your home will also be your carer's home. You cannot expect her to spend all her time off cooped up alone in her bedroom, even if you have given her good facilities. Will you be annoyed by her comings and goings, and by having her friends round, hanging about the kitchen? You also cannot expect her, just because she is on the premises, to do childminding at weekends and evenings without prior arrangement, however tempting it might be to ask.

Don't expect too much from young au pairs. They can be wonderful, but they can also display as much selfishness, laziness and unreliability as many others of their age. Make sure your chosen carer really is comfortable with caring for a small baby, and provide plenty of back-up from relatives and neighbours.

A relative can often provide the most reliable and loving environment for a baby, but we aren't all lucky enough to have a willing mother, mother-in-law or sister who is free to do this. But, if you choose a childcarer carefully, your baby and her carer can have a mutually satisfying and loving relationship that you should encourage without guilt or possessiveness. Remember that if you are having trouble accepting the childcare arrangements that you have made, then so will your child, and you will need to make some changes.

organizing childcare

Choosing the right childcare is obviously the most important decision you will have to make when returning to work, so take your time and really investigate the options available to you. You must also work out well in advance exactly what you want the carer to be responsible for, and agree everything before she starts.

Once you have employed someone, if you ever have the slightest doubt that she is less than fully competent, you must deal with it immediately, however inconvenient, even if it means taking time off work to do so. If, however, you can't find someone with whom you are completely happy, then delay your return to work, or find interim childcare from a friend or relative.

references

Check your proposed carer's references with a person-to-person talk with her previous employer, even if the carer comes through an agency. A written reference is not enough. If there seems to be a problem with doing this when it is suggested, then be suspicious. Most nannies and childminders are decent, honest people, but your baby is too precious for you to be less than thorough. Follow your instincts on this matter.

care options

The different options for your baby's care have already been discussed (see pages 134-35), whether it is live-in, daily care, a relative, childminder or nursery, but you won't really know whether your chosen option suits you until you are back at work. You might find that you need more flexibility than a nine-to-five carer offers, that having someone living with you does not work or that taking your baby back and forth to the childminder each day is too stressful. Your finances are obviously a consideration, but your childcare must work for you as well as for your baby. If you are finding the arrangement leaves you worn out, then be prepared to look for an alternative.

job description

Draw up a list of things you want your baby's carer to do before you interview her. Obviously there can be room for discussion on this, but both of you should know exactly what is expected as being vague can cause problems later on. The list should include your likes and dislikes about childcare, such as your attitude to dummies, how much fresh air you want your baby to have and whether you allow your baby to be left to cry for short periods. Make sure that you and your partner are in agreement too.

as your carer starts work

It is wise to set aside a week before you go back to work when you can be with your chosen carer and see how she and your baby get on together. This helps to iron out any potential problems right at the start and will make you much more confident about leaving your baby in her care.

It is also a good idea to suggest a trial period for both you and your nanny. Be honest about things you are not happy with, and ask her to do the same. But also make it clear that she risks instant dismissal for any form of negligence to your baby.

support

Being alone with a baby can be very isolating, so make sure your carer has avenues of support such as friends or neighbours nearby she can phone for a chat, other nannies in the area or group get-togethers for mothers and nannies with young children.

time off

It can be tiring to do a full week's work then take over childcare at weekends, however much you love your children. Your nanny will definitely need proper time off each week, ideally two days, but try to arrange that you occasionally get a day off too when you don't have to go to work, perhaps by asking a relative to help, so you and your partner can have some time alone together.

Your baby will thrive with a kind and loving carer if you are keen to return to work, as long as your arrangements are carefully planned and monitored.

practical concerns

As the time approaches when you will be leaving your baby to return to work, you should begin to consider all the practical elements of your new life, and try to be prepared for all but the most unexpected eventualities. Many women feel that they lose the ability to think clearly in the months after childbirth, so it is important to write things down and discuss your plans with your partner, so that everyone knows what is going on.

preparing for a live-in carer

You will probably have a carer booked by now (possibly following the advice give on pages 134–37), but you may not have thought about some of the day-to-day details of having someone else in your house, whether part- or full-time. For example, have you got a spare house key for the carer? Have you decided whether you want her to drive your car, and, if so, is it insured for her to do so? If she is living in, is her room ready with sheets and towels, a reading light, a television etc? How will you pay her? And have you written out a list of contact numbers for her, like the doctor, a neighbour and your closest relative, along with yours and your partner's work numbers? There are many things to prepare before your carer starts.

care away from home

Taking your baby to her carer as well as being punctual at work, then doing the reverse journey at the end of the day without panicking or being late, can require a good deal of advance planning.

First you must decide who will do the taking and fetching. This will depend on the location of your childcare in relation to your workplaces, and the actual hour that your and your partner's jobs begin, but try and make the process a joint effort. Perhaps you can deliver her and your partner can pick her up. Leave plenty of time both ends for transport delays and to avoid getting anxious. If your job sometimes requires you to stay a little late, make sure your carer is happy about this. If you take liberties with her good will then the arrangement will not last for long.

You will also have to buy a sturdy bag to hold all your baby's equipment for the day, which will need to include nappies, baby wipes, a change of clothes, bottles and puréed food if she is being weaned, outdoor clothes, her buggy, her favourite blanket for her nap, a few of her toys and all your contact phone numbers.

parenting preferences

If you are involving other people as you bring up your child, then it is essential that there is some consensus about basic parenting decisions, especially at this early stage, when you are planning to let someone else take over your baby's care. It is only going to cause confusion if you say one thing to the carer and your partner says another. For instance, he may think it is fine for your nanny to leave your baby to cry after a feed, while you may be totally opposed to this. He may dislike the thought of your nanny taking your baby to another nanny's house, but you may be happy for her to do this. Sit down together and work out any problem areas, then present yourselves, united, to your baby's carer.

clothes for work

You will hate your pregnancy clothes at this stage. But you might not have got your figure back to its pre-pregnancy glory before you have to go back to work. Give yourself plenty of time to go through your wardrobe and find some suitable work clothes, or buy a couple of new items, so that you aren't hurling clothes about the bedroom in despair on your first week back at work.

breastfeeding If you are breastfeeding, then make sure you have a good supply of nursing bras and breast pads. You will need to take some spare breast pads to work because, for most women, the mere thought of their baby triggers the let-down reflex in their breasts, and milk begins to flow as a result. You should begin to cut down your baby's daytime feeds in the two weeks before you return to work, to allow your milk supply to adjust. Otherwise your breasts will be very full and painful by the end of the working day, and expressing milk at work may prove awkward.

However, if you actually find that expressing milk at work is helpful then feel free to do so and freeze it straight away. By doing this you can be providing breast milk for your baby's feedings on the next day, thereby giving your baby breast milk full-time, while working full-time, although you obviously won't be able to breastfeed at each occasion. It is really up to you what you do and depends on whether you feel strongly about always providing breast milk (see pages 118–19).

back-up arrangements

When you have decided on your day-to-day plan for your return to work, you should also have back-up arrangements in case anything goes wrong. Ask a couple of relatives or friends if they are prepared to step in if there is a problem with the carer. Decide how you will get your baby to her carer if the car breaks down and work out between you and your partner who can leave work more easily if there is an unforeseen crisis. It is always a good idea to leave contact numbers and a spare house key with your neighbours. You will also need to work out what you will do when the carer takes a holiday.

You can never guarantee that things will run smoothly when you are trying to fit so much into your day, but with careful planning you can at least minimize the stress caused by unnecessary chaos. Always remember to ask for the help that you need.

feeling stretched in all directions

There has been an unspoken agreement between the sexes for generations that the man has been allowed to go to work knowing his children are being looked after by his wife. Many women now choose to go back to work after having had children, but it is still rare for the father to stay at home and be the childminder.

Many working mothers have to fit an incredible amount of extra responsibilities into their working day and, as a mother with a job, it will probably still be you who is the main organizer of childcare and the one who does the highest proportion of domestic tasks. The buck, as far as your children are concerned, stops with you. Why is this? Partly because old habits and sociological expectations die hard, and partly because of the iniquitous position of women being paid less than men, so men's jobs are still seen as more important. It is also due to the instinctive child-consciousness women have, perhaps from being the one who actually bears, and breastfeeds, the child.

It is not uncommon, therefore, for women to get up in the morning, get their children dressed and breakfasted, drive them to childcare or school, go on to work, then do the reverse at the end of the day, picking up provisions en route, while the man showers and dresses and goes to work. Blame for this ridiculous division of labour rests with both parties; men are not the villains here, nor should women be the martyrs, but there is absolutely no merit in continuing to live such a lopsided, exhausting existence.

proper division of labour

Before you return to work, organize what is appropriate for you, your partner and your carer to do each day. We all have different strengths and weaknesses so, if you are a bad timekeeper, make delivering your baby to childcare your partner's task. But be flexible; this is new for all of you and you will probably have to compromise to make your days run smoothly. But don't be trapped into cooking and cleaning for your carer. Some women complain that having a live-in nanny is almost like having another child to look after.

getting strong and fit

Many women in the first months after childbirth think so much about their baby that they forget to look after themselves. But the first priority before returning to work is to get physically well and fit so that you have the energy to stay on top of your busy schedule. This can be accomplished with both diet and exercise, but does not require long hours in the gym or restricting your calorie intake. We are talking health here, not thinness.

You may not have had the time for a structured physical exercise programme postnatally, but you should certainly have

Trying to juggle baby, work, social life and relationship can be a tiring and stressful process for anyone, unless you get used to asking those around you for the help you need right from the start.

been doing some gentle stretching and toning exercises, with an emphasis on the stomach and pelvic floor. Postnatal exercises should be begun gently and worked up in strength as your muscle tone returns. You can also begin to walk with your baby in tow. Either strap your newborn into a supportive sling, or put him in a pram, then walk for at least half an hour at a good pace five times a week. Some exercise clubs and swimming pools offer crèches for women with young children too.

Your diet is particularly important at this time. You might be worried about your weight, but you can eat a nutritious diet to recover your energy and strength that is not high in fat. The familiar mantra of lots of fruit, vegetables and wholefood carbohydrates has never been more important. Even if you are alone at home during the day, make sure you eat your meals regularly. Lots of small ones are better than one big one, because your stomach digests small amounts more efficiently, and you don't have the chance to get too hungry and risk bingeing on the first available fast food. And always drink plenty of water, as dehydration from too many caffeine drinks can cause headaches and tiredness. Returning to work will probably be a very challenging time. However, if you get yourself organized right from the start, work out how much, and what kind of support you all need to make it work and retain a sense of humour at the occasional times of chaos, you will find things settle down surprisingly quickly and you will create a new routine for the family.

guilt at being a working mother

It is important that you understand that you will probably feel guilty when you go back to work. Therefore, try not to waste your time fighting it, but recognize it for what it is – a normal human reaction. It doesn't mean that your decision to return to work is wrong, but you will have to deal with your feelings.

Remember that we all feel guilty about something we have done as parents. We feel we should have been more patient, let our baby sleep in our bed with us, have given her more fresh air, not left her to cry so often, or should have breastfed her for longer. Just one article in a newspaper or magazine about parenting can send the best of us into a guilty decline. It is all quite ridiculous, but most of us do have these feelings to some degree so firstly realize that you are not alone. It is also obvious that such guilt can be at a premium if you decide to return to work and leave your precious bundle in the hands of a stranger.

what is your baby missing?

You will feel guilty at first about leaving your baby with her carer. You are sure she will not give her quite the quality of care that you do, and therefore you worry that you are letting your baby down. It is to be hoped that you trust your chosen carer to keep your baby safe, but will she stimulate her enough and give her the mental, physical and social confidence that you would provide? The answer is that she will care for her differently because she is a different person, and this can be a valuable and stimulating extension to your baby's experience. You will be able to tell quickly and easily whether your baby is settled and happy with her carer, and, if she is, then you should leave them to their relationship with confidence.

what are you missing?

You will feel especially guilty when your carer tells you that your baby has been ill or miserable when you were not there to comfort her, or when you miss an important event in her life, such as taking a first step or speaking her first word, because you were sitting behind your desk at the time. This is the downside of being a working mother, but it is inevitable that you will miss many moments in her life, both now and when she goes to school. If you don't want to do this, then you will have to think again about your career, and maybe do part-time work for the few years before she goes to school. But if you have decided to work and you enjoy it, then view the time that you have with her as precious and don't worry about the bits you miss. Your guilt is probably based around concern for the welfare of your child, but she won't be worried about who witnesses her first step will she? Always make sure your carer can contact you, which is not hard in this age of the mobile phone, and ask her to let you know about any significant event in your child's life as soon as it occurs.

quality time

The phrase 'quality time', the 'perfect' time a working mother intends to spend with her child, automatically implies guilt. You can't be with your child for most of the day, so you may be absolutely determined to make up for it when you get home. If you do this, your poor child, who has been pottering about all day playing and doing her own thing as all children like to do, will suddenly be bombarded by games, puzzles, flash cards, and the manic attention of her hitherto absent parent. What she would much rather do is relax and have a cuddle, then return to her previous play, knowing you are there. So stop feeling guilty and just enjoy her.

tiredness and parenting

If you are working a long day, and you get home exhausted only to be faced with various parenting duties such as bathing, feeding and putting your child to bed, you may sometimes feel like a reluctant parent. This will then trigger another bout of guilt. But instead of feeling guilty, why don't you make sure that your child's schedule allows for you to come home and put your feet up with a cup of tea before embarking on the rigours of childcare. Perhaps you could pay your carer to stay an extra half an hour longer than you had originally arranged, or share the tasks with your partner, having one day on, one day off. It can't be stressed enough that your child is a product of both you and your partner, and the care of your child should definitely also be a shared process.

accidents

Sometimes the unthinkable happens, and your baby has an accident when you are not there. This produces understandable guilt, but there are very few parents who are with their children every moment of every day, and an accident is just that, an unforeseen event that may occur at any time. It bears no relation to whether you are working or not. As long as you have taken every precaution to ensure your baby is safe, it is pointless to blame yourself for what has happened. You can choose to wallow in working-mother guilt and make yourself tense and stressed because of it, or you can choose to be confident in the decision that you and your partner have taken about the way your baby is to be brought up, and then enjoy the fact that she is, for the vast majority of the time, happy and well looked after by a loving alternative to you. Your baby will not appreciate the former so be positive.

The various different people that we have around us as children teach us what we know about human nature. If the experiences we have with them are mainly good, we grow up confident in ourselves and in how we relate to others. So don't spend your children's early years feeling guilty that you are not with them every minute of every day.

flexible working

Without the ability to accurately predict how you will feel after the birth of your first baby, you will have set up plans around home and work, which, at the time, seemed perfectly reasonable. The problem is that many women just continue to accept situations that are, in fact, unacceptable, not realizing that they can change them, and as a result end up dispirited. Don't let yourself be one of them.

The work debate is so often centred round the 'to work or not to work' question, but less commonly around the possibilities of working in a different way. It is taking a long time for the male-orientated world of work to change its practices in favour of the ever-growing female workforce. But some of the more enlightened companies are realizing that they are wasting millions every year on training and recruitment if they then do not accommodate the needs of the working mother and therefore lose staff as a result.

Organizations such as New Ways to Work, which researches and promotes flexible work solutions for those with caring responsibilities, and the Equal Opportunities Commission both believe that we should be working towards a family-friendly workplace, where flexible working is accepted practice.

It is really up to working mothers to stop being in thrall to old-fashioned work practices, and to realize that raising children is a shared responsibility between men, women and society in general, and no longer the exclusive domain of women. Statistics show that currently only 57.1 per cent of women are able to work full-time, because they have assumed the responsibility for childcare, but 92.5 per cent of men continue to work. If women want to work in a different way so that they can combine a career with their family, then each of us has to stand up and say so. But first you need to think about what the possible options are and which of them would suit you and your family the best.

changing the way you work

Employers have a duty to seriously consider a request for flexible working for childcare reasons, and can only refuse the request if they have a good business-related reason to justify their refusal. If they insist a working mother works full-time, despite her request to do otherwise, and this insistence puts the woman at a disadvantage because she can no longer work full-time, then the employers could be liable for indirect sex discrimination if the case went to an employment tribunal. However, the woman would need to show that she has a good reason for asking for flexible hours because of her childcare responsibilities. A man would also have a claim for direct sex discrimination if refused part-time work when a woman in his organization was allowed it.

Because a high percentage of jobs have traditionally been done between certain hours of the day, usually nine to five, many of us, both employers and employees alike, assume that this is the way that they always have to be done. Making the leap of faith that this need not be so requires proper time and consideration, and perhaps your employer has never been asked to do this before. However, a survey in 1996 by the Department for Education and Employment found that 71 per cent of the 1311 employers represented offered some form of flexible working arrangements. There are various ways you can work more flexibly to give yourself a better quality of life as a working mother without leaving the job market. If you are unhappy with your way of working you should put your suggestions for alternatives to your employer and see if you can come to some agreement. Think in advance of how to overcome any difficulties your employer might find with your proposed new arrangements.

WORKING ALTERNATIVES

The alternatives to working a full day include:

- Working part-time (see pages 146–47).
- Working flexi-time, which means working the same hours but at different times of the working day. For instance, you could work hours that enable you to be home in time to pick your child up from school.
- Working from home some of the time. This is when you do your job from home for either part of the day or whole days during the week. This possibility has been greatly facilitated by the IT revolution.
- Working shifts that accommodate childcare, so you might work all day Monday and Tuesday, but have Wednesday and Thursday morning off because your carer is engaged on another job. Make sure you are not required to work unpredictable hours or overtime without proper notice if you do shift work.
- Job sharing, where another similarly qualified person will share your job with you (see pages 148–9).

employers against flexibility

The following are some reasons that are commonly given by employers for not allowing working flexibility, but they are unlikely to amount to a good business reason in an employment tribunal. They may say that:

- the job is too senior
- there are no part-time vacancies
- last-minute overtime is essential or
- continuity in the job is crucial.

If your employer gives any of these reasons you may have a claim for indirect sex discrimination.

be clear about what you want

Don't be shy about asking for an alternative working arrangement. Your employer may not have suggested it before because he or she never thought of it, but this doesn't mean that your company will not be open to new ideas that you propose, especially as they might benefit the company as much as you.

part-time work

You may get back to work after the end of your maternity leave to discover that you cannot find reliable childcare to fit in with your full-time, nine-to-five, schedule. Or you might simply find that working the long hours you used to, when you had no other commitments in your life, is now putting you under too much strain. Part-time work could be a good alternative for you.

You may have an unforeseen problem with your childminder, such as the fact that they can only do mornings, or cannot look after your baby on Mondays or Fridays, and any alternative would be too expensive to be viable. Alternatively, you may have difficulty fitting work and your new responsibilities together. Whether your company has, up until now, employed part-time staff or not, they must still consider this possibility seriously. The law on asking for part-time work is the same as for asking for flexible work, a job-share, reduced hours or homeworking: you have a right to ask if new arrangements are needed because of childcare responsibilities and circumstances. Employers also have a duty to consider the request and must have good business-related reasons for refusing or it could be indirect sexual discrimination.

Your employer may say that there is too much work for a part-time employee to do, in which case she has to consider employing another person in a job-share agreement. An argument she might raise against this solution is that two people doing the same job will risk lack of continuity. And whereas this is certainly a possibility if the situation is badly managed, there are simple, practical ways in which two people can liaise about their work to a satisfactory degree (see pages 148–9).

You may be given the excuse by your employer that the firm cannot afford to employ part-timers. Depending on what you do, this is not necessarily the case. The company will not have to pay higher National Insurance contributions by employing you part-time as the costs are worked out as a percentage of your salary, and you can share any equipment essential for your job with another employee also on part-time work if your hours are dovetailed.

A reasonable refusal to allow a female employee to leave at 5.30pm each day might be if a particular business has to stay open late in the evening, for instance a shop or a hairdressing salon that is open until 7pm to catch people on their way home from work. If you were unable to work beyond 5.30pm this would put an unfair burden of work on the other employees in the evening, and bringing someone else in for that hour and a half would not be a practical option. A job-share, however, might be a better solution for that situation.

childcare and part-time work

Securing reliable childcare can be hard under any circumstances, and the flip side of not being able to find someone to look after your children full-time is the problem of finding a carer who wants to work only part-time because that is all your pay allows for, or you have decided you want to spend more time with your children while they are small. You may want to work just two days a week, on Tuesday and Thursday, but your carer will probably need more employment than that, and finding a family who needs childcare for Monday, Wednesday and Friday may not be very easy to do.

It is advisable to find out who is available and for what hours they might care for your baby before talking about new working hours with your employer. You may, however, be able to divide your work into some time at home and some at the office. You may be able to co-opt a relative for one day, and a carer for the other. Your employer may also be happy for you to choose the days in which you work, just so long as you get the work done. You should also ask around your friends and acquaintances to see if any of them would like to share a nanny. There may be someone who, for example, would like to go back to work part-time, but is having trouble finding childcare too.

unpaid overtime

What all part-time workers must be wary of is finding their supposedly part-time hours creeping up to almost full-time hours, while they are still being paid for the shorter hours. It can sometimes be quite difficult changing from full-time to part-time if you stay in the same job, because your work colleagues have become used to you doing a certain workload. Some may resent the fact that you are no longer willing to stay the full hours, especially if the management has not made adequate provision for your work to be done by another worker. If you feel your employers are taking advantage of your good will, suggest they either reduce your workload to one you can manage, or employ another part-time worker to help out.

if your employer refuses

If you have to resign because you and your employer cannot agree on a more flexible working arrangement you may have a claim for indirect sex discrimination. You must apply to an employment tribunal within three months of the incident, and your potential compensation will be based on loss of earnings – the amount awarded depending on how much you normally earn, and on injury to feelings, with amounts ranging from £2000 to £5000.

It is not always easy to stand up for your rights in the job market, especially when you are perhaps less confident because you have been out of the workplace for a while and may be worried about job security. But the only way to make the workplace a more user-friendly place for women trying to raise a family is to be brave enough to negotiate different options.

job-sharing

Job-sharing is another option to consider. Figures from a Department of Trade and Industry survey in 1998 showed that approximately 15 per cent of female employees and 5 per cent of male employees work in job-shares. We all have different strengths and weaknesses, and employing two people in the same job, if they are carefully chosen, offers a broader base of experience and skills.

For example, imagine that two women are employed to manage a canteen on a job-share arrangement. One may be excellent at keeping the accounts and anticipating the quantities of foodstuffs that need to be ordered, while the other may have excellent personnel skills to keep the workforce happy and so can be in charge of hiring and firing. One may like working early in the day because she wants to fetch her special-needs child from school, the other may have a partner who does the school run and is therefore happy to stay until later. This arrangement can often benefit the employer as much as it does the working mother.

Some women might be uneasy about job-sharing on the basis that their colleague could be perceived as better at the work they share than they are, and therefore they constantly feel in competition for their own job. Whereas this is a natural, human reaction, you should see your colleague as facilitating your ability to work, and try to share the tasks out so that each of you is doing what you are best at. If you feel your colleague is being competitive, then talk to her about it and find out why.

negotiating different hours

You have decided you would like to change your hours now that you are a mother, but what is the best way to go about it? Ask yourself the following questions before you approach your employer, personnel manager or union representative:

- How do you actually work at present? Is your work spread evenly over the day, or do you have a time when you are particularly busy? Is this busy period self-imposed or reliant on outside influences? For instance, if you work in a gym your busiest time might be before or after normal working hours, when your clients are on their way to or from their work, and there is little choice in the matter. Or you might work a lot with companies abroad and have to consider the different time zones when you do your business. Decide whether it has to be done this way, or if there are any alternatives.
- Next ask yourself if your job really has to be done by one person or if it could reasonably be shared. Each one of us likes to think of ourselves as indispensable, but is this really true?

- Could you do some of your work from home? The incredible increase in the ease of communication brought about by computers, faxes, email and mobile phones means that we no longer depend on being in the same place all the time. Perhaps you could negotiate two days a week when you work from home, or go in during mornings and work from home in the afternoons.
- What hours can you realistically work? It is easy to be over-optimistic at the beginning of your return to work. You are sure you will be able to cope. But you should also be considering the quality of your family life, not just your working life. If you get tired easily and suffer from minor health complaints then you are probably doing too much.
- How, practically speaking, could you successfully get your job done if you were working different hours? And which hours would they need to be?
- Would your proposal for change suit both you and your employer?

your rights

You still have rights, even if you are doing fewer hours, job-sharing or working different hours from your colleagues.

- Your employer cannot change your job to one with less status just because you are working in a different way.
- You cannot be paid less than the hourly rate you were getting when you were working normal hours. Just because the hours are being worked at different times does not mean they are less valuable.
- You should still get the same holiday entitlement based pro rata on the hours that you work.
- If you do negotiate a change in your hours, you must realize that you have no legal right to your old full-time job back, unless your employer agrees, so think carefully about what you want before approaching them.

benefits

As you can see, suggesting a more flexible approach to your working hours, and sharing your job with someone else, can benefit your company too. So take the view that you might be doing everyone a favour by working to your satisfaction. And if it doesn't work out you can go on to try one of the other options (subject to negotiation with your employer and taking into account that he is allowed to justify refusing if it would be hard to run the business as a result). As your children grow and the general needs of the family change, so too can your work.

FLEXIBLE COMPANIES

The more enlightened companies who have begun to employ much more flexible working arrangements for their workforce have found it to be very beneficial. Since one company introduced it, the number of women who returned from maternity leave rose from 7 per cent to over 50 per cent. Another company states that they have saved themselves £1m in the five years since they started the scheme, in the areas of training, recruitment and productivity.

bringing work closer to home

You might decide now you have a baby that the best compromise as far as work is concerned is to work from home, either by being self-employed or by doing part- or full-time work for an employer. Working this way will dispense with the need for regular outside babycare, will mean you have flexible working hours to suit yourself and it also avoids the headache of travelling to your workplace.

Such flexibility in where and how you work is a great idea. However, trying to work and look after a baby at home at the same time is not always very successful, and you might find yourself working late into the evenings when your child is in bed to make up the time. This will mean that you get overtired, and you still may not manage to do enough work to maintain a regular income. Even if it is only for a few hours every day, it is often best to try to get someone to come in and take over your baby duties so that you can get on with your own work unimpeded.

being self-employed

Before you decide to resign from your job and go freelance, there are some serious questions to ask yourself.

- Are you self-motivated enough to make working from home a feasible option?
- Can you build up enough work to earn a regular income and, if so, how will you do it?
- Is your house suitable to accommodate both your family and your work?
- Will you get lonely and miserable without work colleagues to chat to?
- What will it cost to establish yourself and do you have the money available?
- How many hours of childcare might you need to get your work done? The au pair option is often suitable as they are not expensive and usually have the afternoon off.

If you have skills that you can develop to create your career at home, such as becoming a writer, designer, researcher, therapist or accountant, then this is the ideal arrangement for coping with the first years of your child's life. But organization is key, and you should set aside a proper work space, not one that has to be cleared away every evening, and make sure you ignore domestic tasks such as washing and hoovering as well as social invitations during 'working hours'. Just because you are working from home and your time is more flexible does not mean that your job has become any less important.

considering your family

One of the problems with working from home is that you are perpetually in your work environment, even in the evenings when your partner comes home. This leaves you open to the possibility of not being able to switch off, which will mean your work begins to impinge on your time with your partner and child.

You may be pressured to take work phone calls in the evenings or early mornings, have work colleagues dropping round or delivering things out of working hours or have people expecting you to work at weekends. You might also be tempted to nip back into your study late at night to solve a work problem that has been bothering you. This sort of behaviour is seldom tolerated for any length of time by those around you, and will also put an unnecessary strain on you.

Learn to create firm parameters for your work and family time. Tell those you work with that you are not available outside work hours and do not work weekends. Find ways to wind down after your day and keep that study door firmly shut outside the times you have allocated as your working day. If you can afford it, have a separate business phone, and switch it to the answer machine when you are not working.

working close to home

If you are not actually thinking of working from home, another consideration is changing jobs so that you are working closer to home. The location of your job has probably been of little concern to you up until now. You may have had an irritating journey back and forth, but you could handle it. Now that you have a baby and are thinking of returning to work, the length and convenience of your journey becomes more of an issue. Your baby clinic will also be situated near to where you live, and visits there will be difficult if you are working a long way from home.

If you do not have home-based childcare you will have to add on the travelling time to deliver your baby to the childminder or the nursery, and you may begin to find that you are spending your whole day rushing around. You may not have the option, depending what your job is, but, if you can, it is worth considering getting work closer to home. The difference it might make to your day could be the difference between continuing to work and giving it all up because of stress. Ask around and see if there are any local alternatives to the job you do now.

If your job is not one that you are willing to change, then there is also the possibility of moving closer to your work. This might seem like an unnecessary upheaval, but if you are thinking of working there for the foreseeable future you are going to have to do that daily round trip to childminder and work and back again for some years to come. It is worth sorting it out before you get worn down by the extra strain your frantic schedule is imposing upon you.

Work is work whether you are a mother or not, and no one will accept shoddy results just because you have a baby. However, the conditions in which you do your work can make the difference between you being half-hearted or highly successful. So do what you can to make your work arrangements as helpful to you as possible.

working breaks

Aside from changing to flexible hours within a regular work structure when your baby is small, there are some actual career and employment breaks available from some employers, depending on the type of work you do and possibly your level of seniority. These might fit in well with the early years of your child's life.

Such breaks are periods in which you do not work, but your job is still your job and you are expected to return to it at the end of the break. The snag is that the time off is usually unpaid or only partly paid, so you would have to have an alternative source of income to be able to take advantage of these breaks.

career breaks

These can be for as little as three months, or as much as five years, are unpaid and in most cases require the employee to have worked for at least 12 months for the company in question. Many companies operate these schemes with varying entitlements and lengths of time off.

You would be expected to return to the same job, or at least a similar one, at the end of your leave, but re-employment is not always guaranteed, and often you will be expected to return on a six-month trial period, or undertake some additional training, depending on how long you have been absent, to ensure you are up-to-date with your job.

Some companies also require that you work a certain number of days each year, which are paid at your normal rate, as part of the deal. These days could be around two weeks that are spread over a one-day-a-month schedule.

The advantage of taking an extended career break, rather than just resigning and then reapplying for another job when you are ready to return to work, is that you have a reasonable level of job security. You should be aware, however, that these breaks may not enhance your career prospects, and you will probably lose your pension rights. Nevertheless, such schemes are becoming increasingly popular as a way for women to be at home until their children begin nursery or formal education. If your company does not run a career break scheme, then suggest that they consider doing so.

sabbaticals

The age at which women are having their first baby is rising all the time, with the proportion of women having their first child at the age of 35 or over up from 4.5 per cent in 1988 to 11 per cent in 1998. (Statistics taken from a Labour Force Survey, Great Britain, 1999.) The mean age for first babies also rose from 25.1 in 1988 to 26.9 in 1998. Because sabbaticals are time off given by employers usually as a reward for continuous service over a lengthy period of time, older mothers are increasingly being able to use them to extend their maternity leave.

Traditionally most sabbaticals are offered in the teaching and academic arena. Some are paid, others are not. Some employers apply no restrictions about how the time is used, while others require the employee to pursue research or enhance their education in some way during their time off. Academics, for example, often use this time to write books, but this can often be done at home and certainly in your own time. Around 20 per cent of employers offer sabbaticals, and these breaks apply to men as much as to women, so perhaps your partner could take a sabbatical around the time of your baby's birth and help you ease back into your own career by providing proper back-up at home.

term-time working

Working mothers often envy teachers their holiday breaks, but this term-time scheme, which can apply to men as well, is a possible alternative when your children are in full-time education as sporadic care to cover the holiday breaks can be a nightmare to organize, whether you are a full-time or part-time worker. You are allowed to take unpaid leave from your job, without the risk of losing it and with normal contractual expectations for your return, for around 13 weeks a year, taken in the school holidays. Your annual four weeks' leave will be included in these 13 weeks, so you are gaining at least eight weeks of unpaid leave. As with sabbaticals, you may be required to go in to work for a pre-arranged day here and there during your time off.

reduced hours scheme

A reduced hours scheme, or voluntary reduced work time (called V-time), although not a complete break, can amount to almost the same thing. Women are enabled to reduce their working hours when they return to work after maternity leave to a minimum of around 16 hours a week (company policies vary), taken flexibly, gradually increasing them to their previous level over a six-month period. You will be paid pro rata for the hours that you work. V-time is an increasingly popular scheme in the United States and is becoming more so in the UK too. One word of warning though: along with part-time and flexi-time working, it seems that you could run the risk of being expected to do more than your hours allow for.

These alternative time-off schemes are worth investigating, even if your employer has no such provision for them currently in place. There is no right to such arrangements, but a refusal could be indirect sex discrimination if it cannot be justified by the employer. In all areas of work these schemes are beginning to gain ground as employers realize that women need every incentive in order to combine childcare and work to their own satisfaction. And a lot of companies are acknowledging that the schemes are useful ways of reducing wastage from lost recruitment and training (see box on page 149).

time out for you and your partner

How many times have you heard the depressing words: 'We haven't had a holiday alone in the 10 years since the children were born'? A holiday soon after you have given birth is definitely unrealistic, but it is the philosophy behind the statement that is the problem.

When you become parents you also become a family, but that doesn't mean you have to throw away your separate relationship with your partner. Finding time as a couple may not be easy, but it also isn't impossible; you just have to recognize its importance and work at making time for yourselves.

and baby makes three

Your baby sleeps in your bed and everything you do centres round him, even if you attempt a candlelit dinner for two in the kitchen, as the baby monitor blinks and crackles by your side. This is all very normal, and it is sensible to realize that for the first few months your baby will take priority over your relationship with your partner, so there's no point in fighting it. But as your baby gets older and more independent, you might be in danger of continuing the habit.

If you then return to work and your time is even more limited, a separate relationship with your partner can fade quietly and sadly into the background. Don't let this happen.

start small

Extravagant weekends in hotels or weeks away together are probably too ambitious to start with, unless you have willing full-time childcare and are able to afford such luxuries. But you can go out to dinner together or, if money is tight, give your baby to his grandparents or some friends and have a cosy night in. You can arrange to meet your partner for lunch when you go back to work, or for a quick drink afterwards, before going home to relieve your carer. Alternatively, join the same gym. Try to have at least some time together each week that is away from the children. And don't spend the whole time discussing the nanny or the pros and cons of different schools. Remember what you used to talk about before you became parents.

social life

Again, your social life will have to go on hold for the first few months after childbirth, until you are feeling fit enough to cope with later evenings and organizing childcare. But don't let the baby become an excuse for not going out and enjoying your friends' company. Most people are quite happy to accommodate a baby in the spare room during a dinner party, or to tuck a toddler in with their own child for a few hours. Obviously it isn't sensible to do this night after night, but once a week could be fun for your children and it will also be a huge relief for you to be able to have a normal social life again.

don't waste your time

One of the problems with parenting, especially if both parents work full-time, is how easy it is to spoil your time together because you haven't worked out how to share the parenting tasks properly. There you are, alone together, your precious offspring tucked up safely in bed, and all you can think of to say is 'Why didn't you get back in time for his bath?' or 'You forgot to buy nappies again.' It sounds petty, doesn't it, but arguing about the children is all too common. And it won't get better as the children get older unless you address it from the start. If you find yourself falling into a pattern of bickering, take a deep breath and sit down together to rework your child-rearing plans. After all, you are both on the same side, and the important thing is that your child gets the best upbringing your joint input can manage. So try not to waste the time you have together on futile disagreements.

time for yourself

Time to yourself after your baby is born can disintegrate into nothing, particularly if this is not your first child, unless you are careful. You will find that you put your baby to sleep and your toddler wakes up, and vice versa; you feed your baby and your toddler wants his supper; you've just got the pair of them down to sleep and then your partner comes home and they wake up because they hear him. Or you might drop them off safely with the childminder and then go and do a day's work. When, exactly, do you have time when you are allowed to think of no one but yourself?

Nobody else will offer to find this time for you, so you will have to arrange it yourself. And don't feel guilty about doing so. For a start, take turns with your partner at the weekend to lie in. Insist that whoever is in charge of the children takes them out of the house for at least an hour in the morning.

Get your children used to entertaining themselves from an early age. There is nothing more depressing than parents who are slaves to their children's every whim, and nothing is worse for the children too.

Ask your partner to babysit one night a week and take a class or go out with your girlfriends. And why not ask your parents or parents-in-law to come on holiday with you so that you can occasionally go and lie on the beach or do something with your partner while they look after the children? Remember that your and your partner's individual needs are as essential to the happy running of the family as your child's requirements are. And no child will develop into a happy and successful adult, what's more, if he has never had to consider the needs of others, or the general good of the family. Family life is a complex balance, but never forget that it is made up of individuals that all need equal consideration. And yes, that does include you!

glossary

Abortion Also called miscarriage, the delivery of the foetus before the 28th week of pregnancy, either spontaneous or medically induced.

Amniocentesis Test for foetal abnormalities such as Down's syndrome.

Amniotic fluid Fluid surrounding baby in womb.

Braxton Hicks contractions Mostly weak contractions which take place throughout pregnancy.

Breech presentation Baby is lying with his bottom down in the uterus, instead of his head.

Caesarean section Delivery of baby through a surgical incision in the mother's abdomen, either under general anaesthetic or an epidural.

Cervix Ring of muscle at the neck of the womb which dilates at the beginning of labour.

Chorionic villi Tiny protrusions around the fertile egg which help it embed in the side of the womb.

Chorionic villus sampling Test where a sample of chorionic villi is obtained either through a needle inserted into the woman's abdomen and into the womb, or via a thin tube through the cervix.

Chromosomes Coiled ribbons of DNA containing genetic material that decides how the body develops and functions. We have 23 pairs in every body cell.

Colostrum Breastmilk produced in the first few days after birth that is particularly rich in proteins and antibodies.

Contractions Tensing and flexing of the muscles of the womb, most intense during labour, which push the baby out and through the birth canal.

Diabetes A condition where the body fails to metabolize glucose. Sugar in the urine and blood is an indicator.

Dilation Opening of the cervix during labour.

Domino scheme A structure of antenatal care and delivery coordinated by hospital and midwife.

Down's syndrome A congenital abnormality caused by chromosomal disorder resulting in specific facial characteristics and mental retardation.

Ectopic pregnancy A pregnancy that develops outside the womb, often in the fallopian tube, which results in termination.

EDD The estimated date of delivery of the baby.

Electronic foetal monitoring Continuous electronic monitoring of the baby during labour.

Embryo The fertilized egg up to the 12th week of pregnancy, when it is then termed a foetus.

Epidural anaesthetic Used in labour, it numbs the body from the waist down through injection into the space around the spine.

Episiotomy Surgical cut to the perineum to make room for the baby's head to pass through.

Fallopian tubes Tubes on either side of the womb assisting the egg's journey from ovary to womb.

Foetus The baby after 12 weeks of pregnancy.

Forceps delivery Delivery of the baby with the assistance of surgical forceps.

Hormone Chemical substances produced by the endocrine system and other glands that affect the body's metabolism and general function.

Hypertension High blood pressure.

Incompetent cervix When the cervix is weak and does not remain closed to the end of the pregnancy.

Induction Artificial stimulation of labour.

Intravenous Delivery of drugs/fluids directly into vein.

Lanugo Covering of fine hair on the baby's body.

Lochia Blood and pinkish discharge from vagina after delivery.

Oedema Fluid retention, usually detected when ankles and fingers swell.

Ovulation Time when egg is released from ovary.

Oxytocin A hormone that stimulates labour.

Pelvic floor Muscles supporting womb, bladder and rectum.

Placenta Organ that grows on the wall of the womb and supports the foetus during pregnancy.

Pre-eclampsia Pre-eclampsia and pre-eclamptic toxaemia are life-threatening conditions for both mother and baby if not treated, in which the pregnant woman has high blood pressure, oedema and albumin in the urine. (Eclampsia is a more severe form, now rare because pre-eclampsia is treated fast.)

Progesterone Hormone increasing in production during pregnancy. Can affect mood and emotions.

Rhesus factor When the mother's blood is Rhesus negative blood and her first baby's Rhesus positive, Rhesus disease might affect subsequent babies unless an injection of gamma globulin is given to the mother.

Rubella (German measles) A virus that can cause foetal abnormalities or miscarriage if contracted in the first 12 weeks of pregnancy.

Serum screening test Blood test to measure maternal levels of hormones and proteins. Results may indicate a neural tube defect in the baby, such as spina bifida.

SIDS, or cot death Unforeseen and unexplained death of a baby. A smoky environment, lying the baby on its stomach and overheating may all be risk factors.

Spina bifida A neural tube defect causing deformity of the baby's spinal cord.

Stillbirth When the baby is born dead after the 28th week of pregnancy.

SUDI Unforeseen death in infants, either with identifiable causes or not.

Termination A medically induced abortion.

Toxoplasmosis A parasite found in cat faeces which can cause blindness in the baby.

Ultrasound scan An image built from bouncing high-frequency sound waves off the foetus, used to monitor foetal development.

Umbilical cord Cord connecting baby to the placenta.

Uterus The womb.

Vertex presentation Also called cephalic presentation, the head-down position of the baby before delivery.

Vernix Waxy coating to the foetus's skin during pregnancy to protect him from the amniotic fluid.

useful organizations

Association of Breastfeeding Mothers, PO Box 207, Bridgwater, Somerset TA6 7YT
Tel: 020 7813 1481

Association for Postnatal Illness, 25 Jerdan Place, London SW6 1BE
Tel: 020 7386 0868

Association of Spina Bifida and Hydrocephalus, ASBAH, 42 Park Road, Peterborough PE1 2UQ
Tel: 01733 555988

Cancer and Leukaemia in Childhood Trust
King Square, Bristol BS2 8JH
Tel: 0117 924 8844

Cystic Fibrosis Trust, 11 London Road, Bromley BR1 1BY
Tel: 020 8464 7211

Down's Syndrome Association, 155 Mitcham Road, London SW17 9PG
Tel: 020 8682 4001

Equal Opportunities Commission, Arndale Centre, Arndale House, Manchester M4 3EQ
Tel: 0161 833 9244

Foundation for the Study of Infant Deaths/Cot Deaths Research and Support, FSID, 14 Halkin Street, London SW1X 7DP
Tel: 020 7235 0965/Helpline: 020 7235 1721

Genetic Interest Group, GIG, Farringdon Point, Farringdon Road, London EC1M 3JB
Tel: 020 7430 0090/0161 833 9244

Gingerbread, 16-17 Clerkenwell Close, London EC1R 0AA
Tel: 020 8464 7211

Haemophilia Society, Chesterfield House, 385 Euston Road, London NW1 3AU
Tel: 020 7380 0600

Health and Safety Executive, Broad Lane, Sheffield S3 7HQ
Infoline: 0541 545500

Independent Midwives Association, Nightingale Cottage, Shamblehurst Lane, Botley, Hampshire SO32 2BY

La Leche League of Great Britain, Box BM 3424, London WC1N 3XX
Tel: 020 7242 1278

Law Centres Federation
Duchess House, 18 Warren Street, London W1T 5LR
Tel: (020) 7387-8570

Maternity Alliance, 45 Beech Street, London EC2P 2LX
Tel: 020 7588 8582

Meet-a-Mum-Association, MAMA, 14 Willis Road, Croydon CR0 2XX
Tel: 020 8771 5595

Miscarriage Association, c/o Claton Hospital, Northgate, Wakefield, West Yorkshire WF1 3JS
Tel: 01924 200799

Multiple Births Foundation, Queen Charlotte's and Chelsea Hospital, Goldhawk Road, London W6 0XG
Tel: 020 8383 3519

National AIDS Helpline: 0800 567 123

National Association of Citizens Advice Bureaux, NACAB, 115-123 Pentonville Road, London N1 9LZ
Tel: 020 7833 2181

National Childbirth Trust, NCT, Alexandra House, Oldham Terrace, London W3 6NH
Tel 020 8992 8637

The National Deafblind and Rubella Association, SENSE, 11-13 Clifton Terrace, London N4 3SR
Tel: 020 7272 7774/Helpline: 0208 991 0513

New Ways to Work, 309 Upper Street, London N1 2TY
Helpline: 020 7226 4026

One Parent Families, 255 Kentish Town Road, London NW5 2LX
Tel: 020 7267 1361

Parentline, Endway House, The Endway, Hadleigh, Benfleet, Essex SS7 2AN
Helpline: 01702 559900/Office: 01702 554782

Pre-eclampsia Society, PETS, 17 South Avenue, Hullbridge, Essex SS5 6HA
Tel: 01702 232533

Stationery Office Publishing, St. Crispins, Duke Street, Norwich, Norfolk NR3 1PD
Tel: 01603 622211

Stillbirth and Neonatal Death Society, SANDS, 28 Portland Place, London W1N 4DE
Tel: 020 7436 5881

Toxoplasmosis Trust, 61-71 Collier Street, London N1 9BE
Tel: 020 7713 059

Twins and Multiple Births Association, TAMBA, PO Box 30, Little Sutton, South Wirral L66 1TH
Tel: 0870 121 4000/01732 868000

index

acknowledgements

Many thanks go to my family and all my friends, the Mitchell Beazley team, Claire Musters, Emily Wright and both the American and British consultants for their patience and support during the writing of *Working Woman's Pregnancy*.

bibliography

Hunter, Adriana, *The Queen Charlotte's Hospital Guide to Pregnancy and Birth*, London: Vermilion, 1998.
Stoppard, Dr Miriam, *Conception, Pregnancy and Birth*, London: Dorling Kindersley, revised 1999.
Kitzinger, Sheila, *The New Pregnancy and Childbirth*, London: Penguin, 1997.
Curtis, Glade B, *Your Pregnancy Week by Week*, Dorset: Element, reissued 1999.
Brewer, Dr Sarah, *I Want to Have a Baby?* London: Kyle Cathie, 1999.
Difiore, Judy, *The Pregnancy Exercise Book*, Dublin: New Leaf, 2000.
Leach, Penelope, *Your Baby and Child*, London: Penguin 1997.
Kohner, Nancy and Mares, Penny, *Having a Baby*, London: BBC publications, 1997.
Bovo, Mary Jane, *The Family Pregnancy*, New York: Donald I. Fine, 1994.
Health and Safety Executive Guides for Employers of New and Expectant Mothers, HSE books, 1997.
Maternity Alliance publications on the rights and benefits of parents and their employers, 2000.

picture credits

Front cover: Mother & Baby Picture Library/Ian Hooten

2 Mother & Baby Picture Library/Sean Knox; 6–7 Mother & Baby Picture Library/Ian Hooten; 11 Mother & Baby Picture Library/Ian Hooten; 12 Mother & Baby Picture Library/Ian Hooten; 19 gettyone stone/Joe Polillio; 20–21 Mother & Baby Picture Library/Paul Mitchell; 24 Science Photo Library/BSIP Dr LR; 31 Mother & Baby Picture Library/Ian Hooten; 33 Science Photo Library/BSIP Barrelle; 36 Mother & Baby Picture Library/Paul Mitchell; 47 Mother & Baby Picture Library/Paul Mitchell; 50 Mother & Baby Picture Library/David Levine; 55 Mother & Baby Picture Library; 65 Science Photo Library/Taeke Henstra/Petit Format; 68–69 Science Photo Library/Gaillard, Jerrican; 86–87 Mother & Baby Picture Library/Ian Hooten; 101 Science Photo Library/Joseph Nettis; 102 Mother & Baby Picture Library/Ian Hooten; 104–105 Mother & Baby Picture Library/Ian Hooten; 111 Image Bank/M Regine; 124 gettyone stone/Jonathan Morgan; 126–127 gettyone stone/Tony May; 137 gettyone stone/Laurence Monneret; 141 gettyone stone/Simon McComb